PIANO VOCAL GUITAR

CHRIS TOMLIN
LOVE RAN RED

T0056114

ISBN 978-1-4950-0571-8

HAL•LEONARD®
CORPORATION
7777 W. BLUEMOUND RD. P.O. BOX 13819 MILWAUKEE, WI 53213

Visit Hal Leonard Online at
www.halleonard.com

GREATER

Words and Music by BEN FIELDING,
CHRIS TOMLIN, MATT REDMAN
and ED CASH

With praise

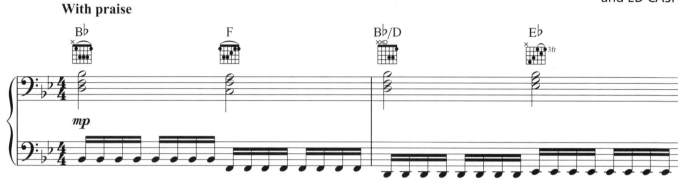

From

Him, through Him, and to Him are __ all things. __ To

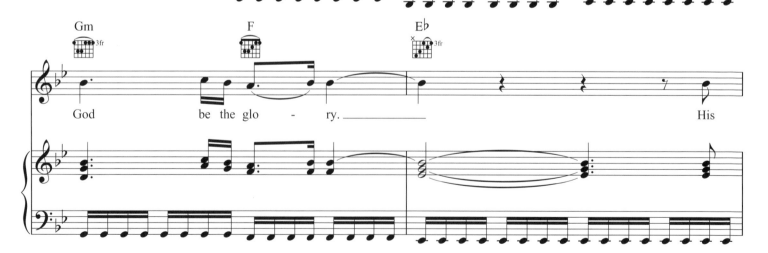

God be the glo - ry. _____ His

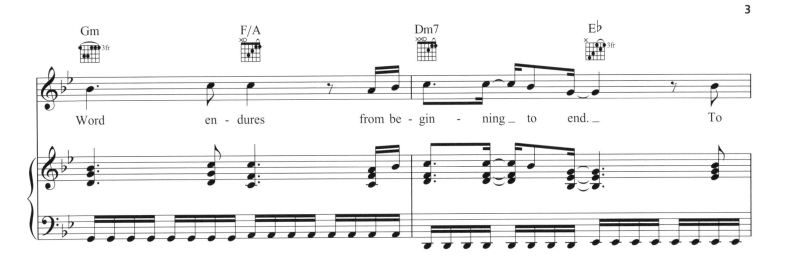

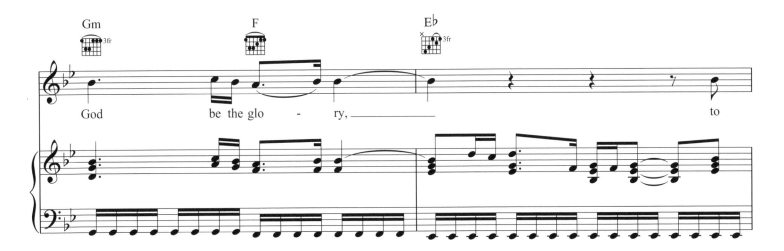

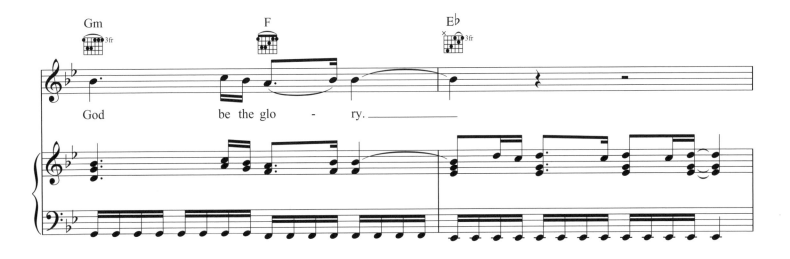

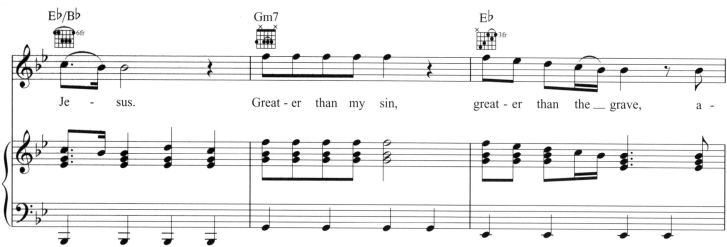

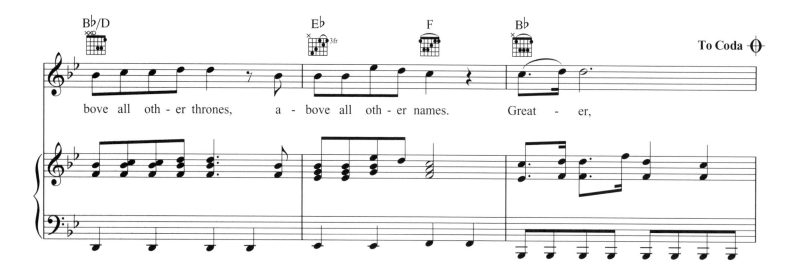

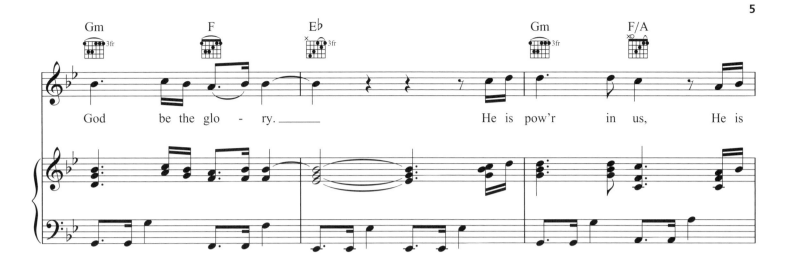

God be the glo - ry. _____ He is pow'r in us, He is

strength for _____ the weak. _____ To God be the glo - ry, _____

_____ to God be the glo - ry.

Great - er is the One who lives in _____ me.

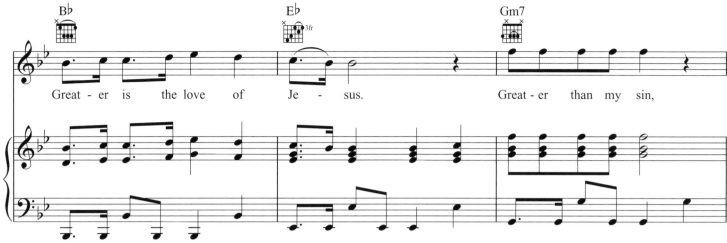

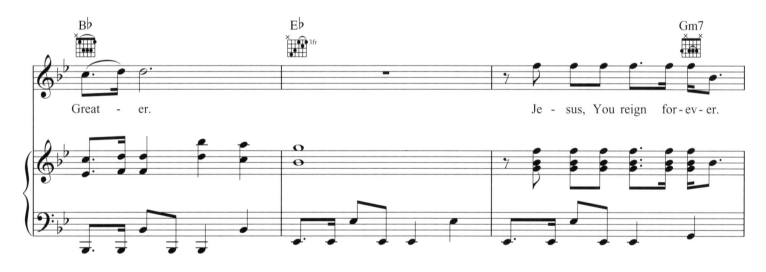

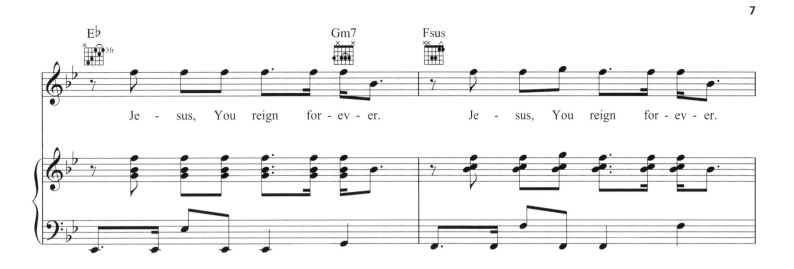

Je - sus, You reign for - ev - er. Je - sus, You reign for - ev - er.

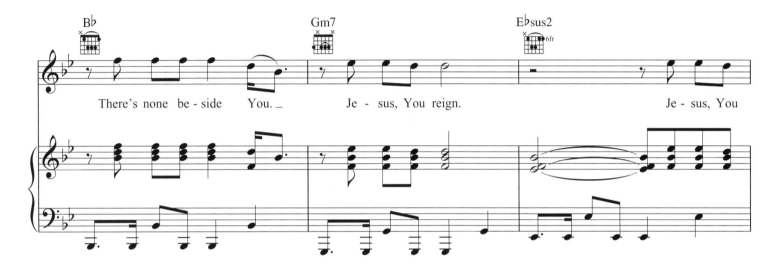

There's none be - side You. _ Je - sus, You reign. Je - sus, You

reign. Great - er is the One who lives in _____ me.

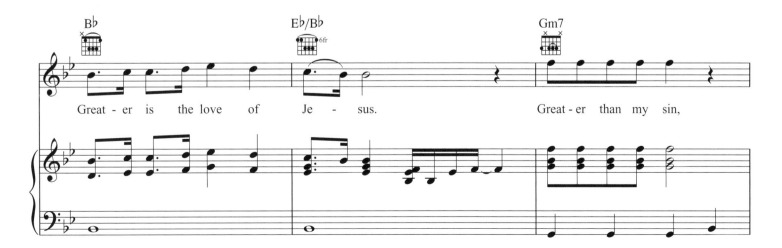

Great - er is the love of Je - sus. Great - er than my sin,

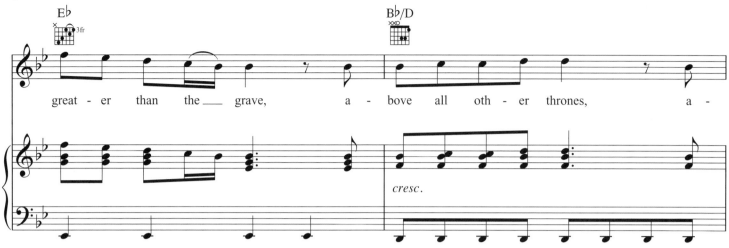

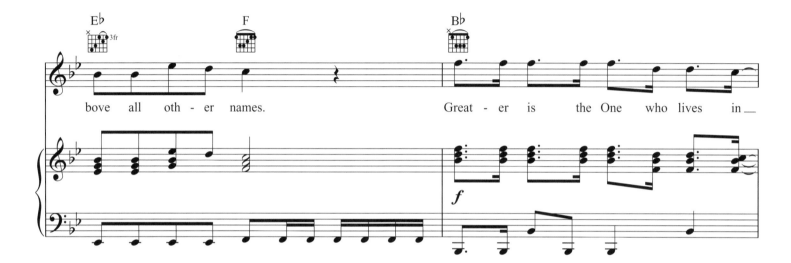

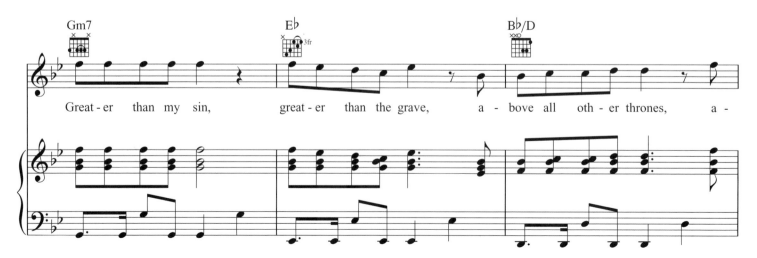

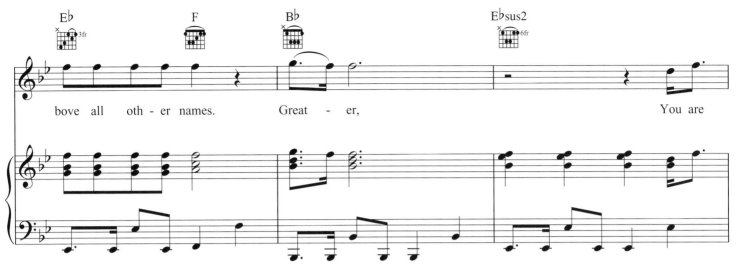

bove all oth - er names. Great - er, You are

great - er. You are great - er.

You are great - er. _____

WATERFALL

Words and Music by CHRIS TOMLIN
and ED CASH

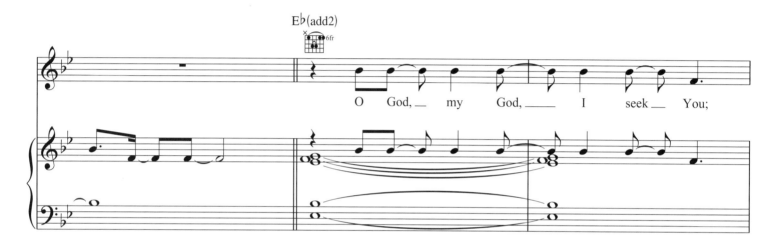

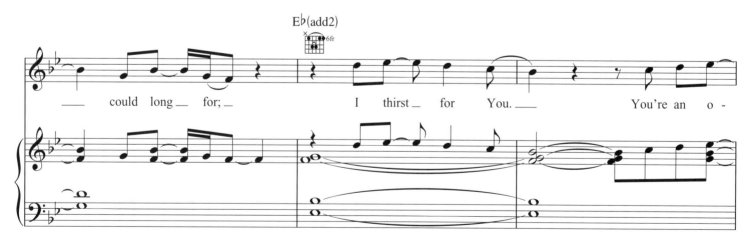

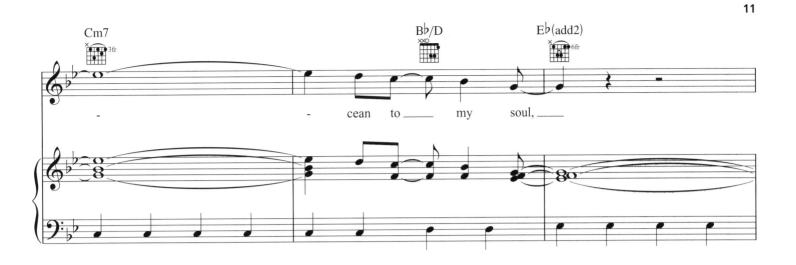

- cean to ___ my soul, ___

to ___ my soul. ___

gradual cresc.

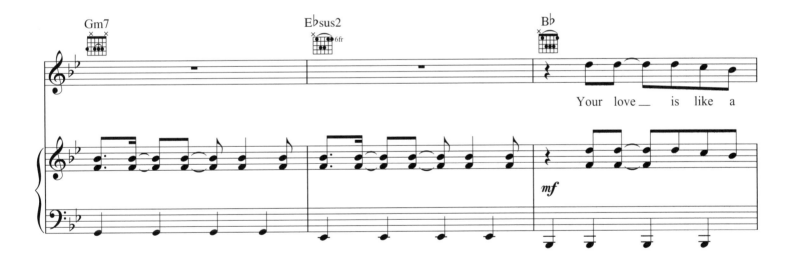

Your love ___ is like a

mf

wa - ter - fall,   wa - ter - fall,   run - ning wild ___ and ___ free. ___

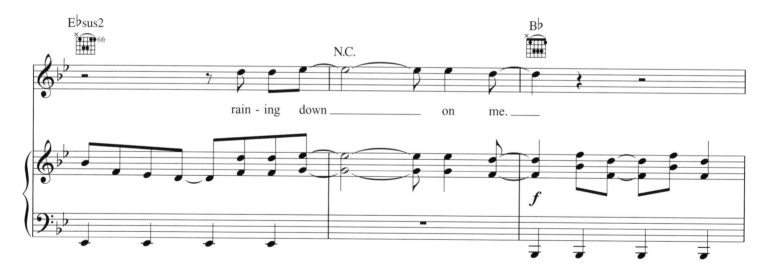

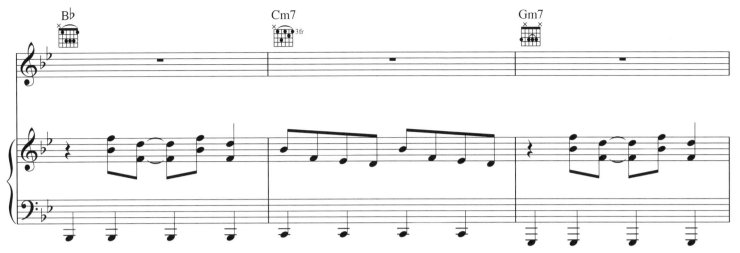

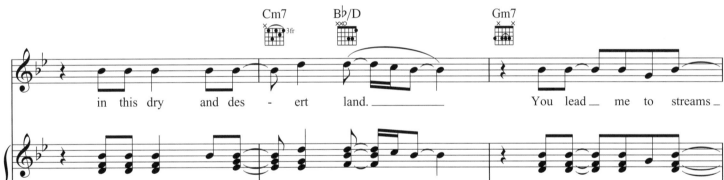

O God, __ my God, __ I seek __ You

in this dry and des - ert land. _____ You lead __ me to streams __

__ of mer - cy once a - gain. __ You're an o -

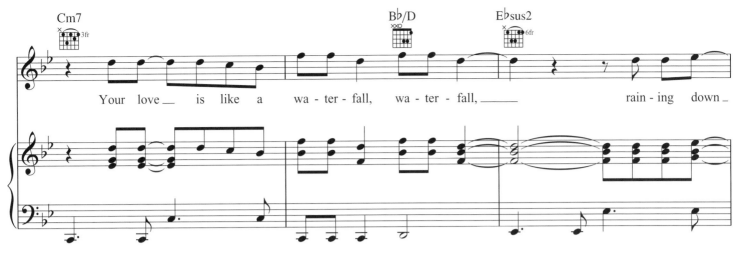

Your love __ is like a wa -ter - fall, wa -ter - fall, _____ rain - ing down __

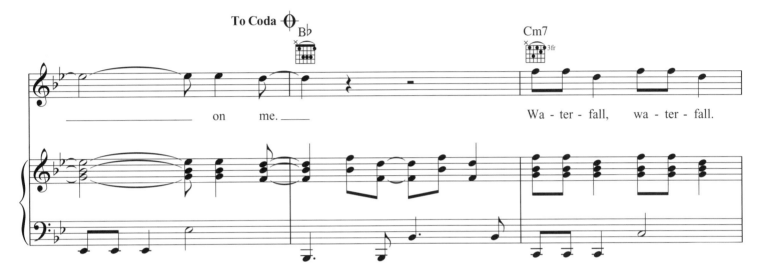

_____ on me. ____ Wa - ter - fall, wa - ter - fall.

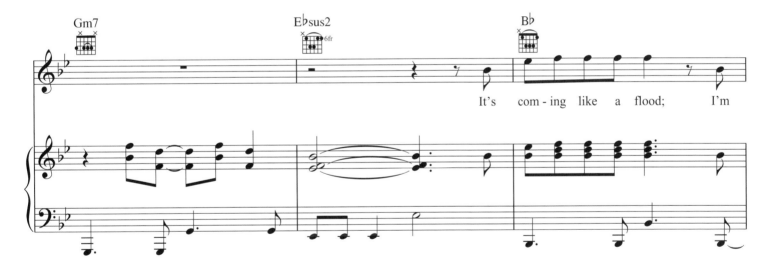

It's com - ing like a flood; I'm

danc - ing in the rain. Ev - 'ry - thing I've done is cov - ered __ in riv - ers __ of

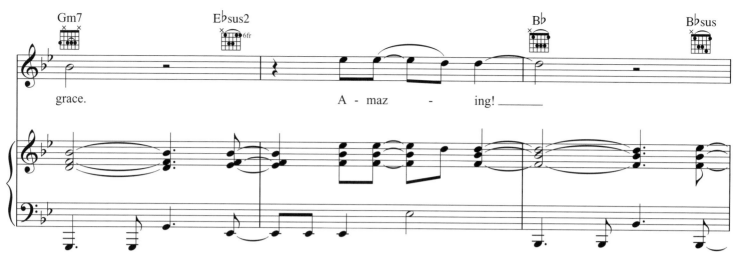

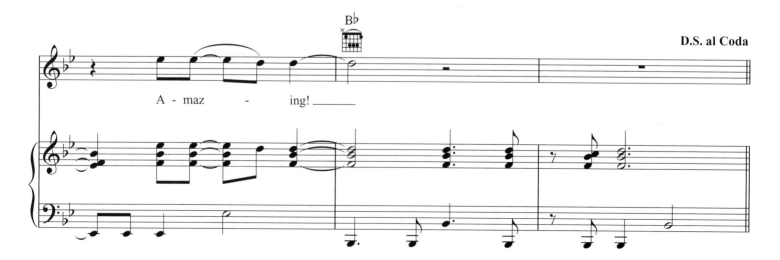

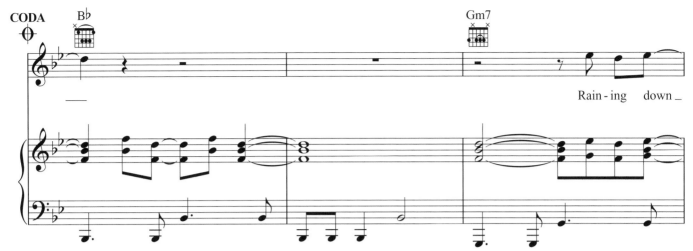

CODA

Rain - ing down

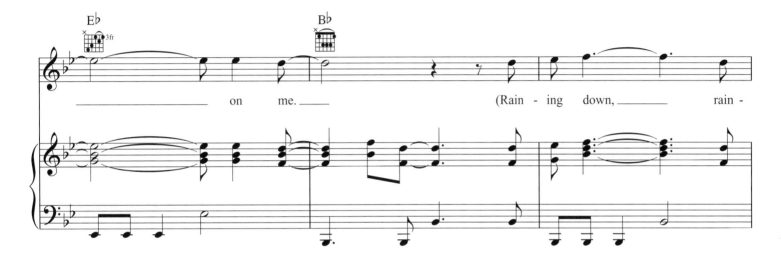

on me. (Rain - ing down, rain -

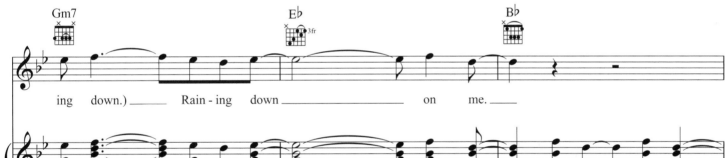

ing down.) Rain - ing down on me.

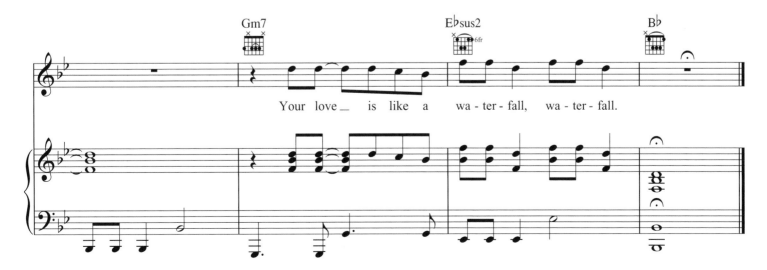

Your love is like a wa - ter - fall, wa - ter - fall.

AT THE CROSS
(Love Ran Red)

Words and Music by MATT REDMAN,
JONAS MYRIN, CHRIS TOMLIN,
ED CASH and MATT ARMSTRONG

love I've ev - er ___ found comes like a flood, comes flow -

- ing down. ___ At the cross, at the cross I sur -

ren - der my life. I'm in awe of You, I'm in awe of You. Where Your

love ran ___ red and my sin washed white, I owe all to You, I owe

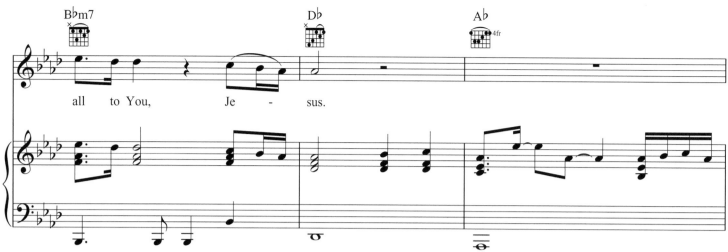

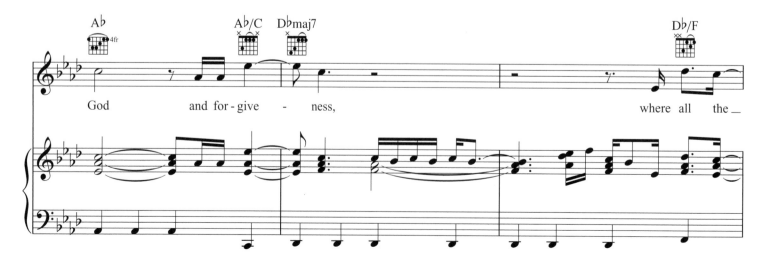

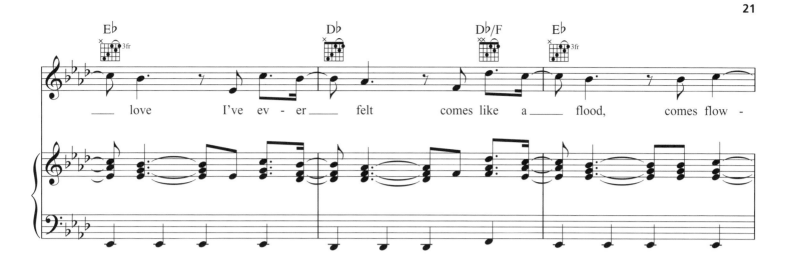

love I've ev - er ___ felt comes like a ___ flood, comes flow -

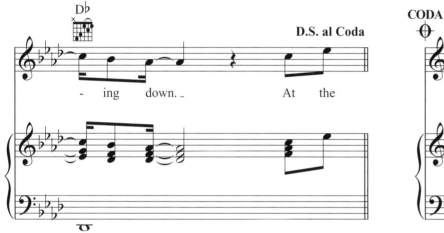

- ing down. ___ At the

D.S. al Coda

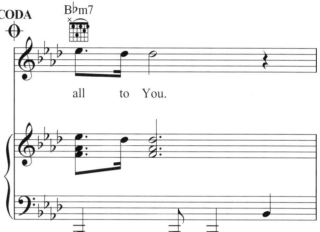

all to You.

Here my hope is found, here on ho - ly ground. Here I bow ___ down,

here I bow ___ down. Here, arms o - pen wide, here You saved my life. ___

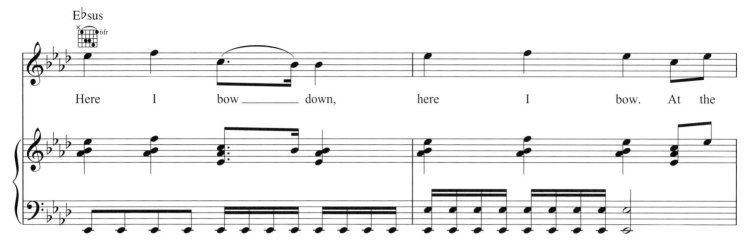

Here I bow _____ down, here I bow. At the

cross, at the cross I sur- ren - der my life. I'm in awe of You, I'm in

awe of You. Where Your love ran red and my sin washed white, I owe

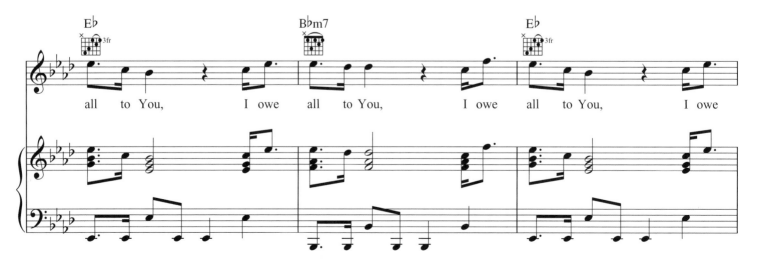

all to You, I owe all to You, I owe all to You, I owe

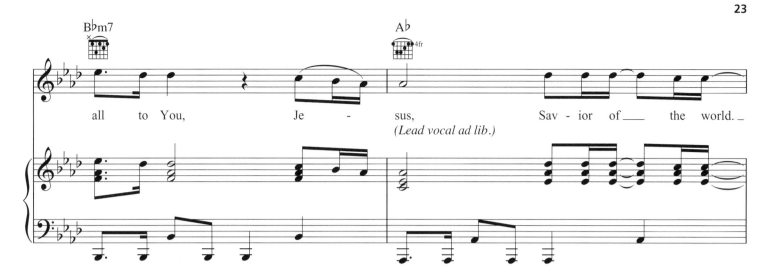

all to You, Je - sus, Savior of ___ the world. ___

(Lead vocal ad lib.)

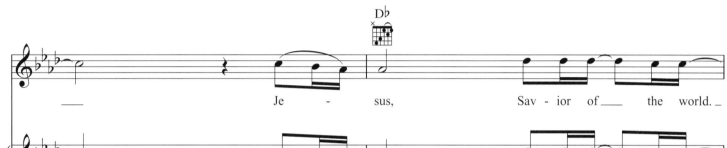

Je - sus, Savior of the world. ___

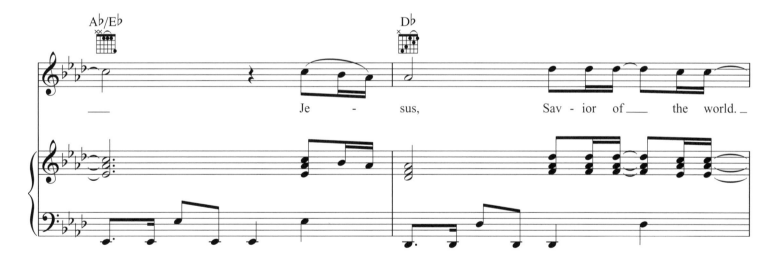

___ Je - sus, Savior of ___ the world. ___

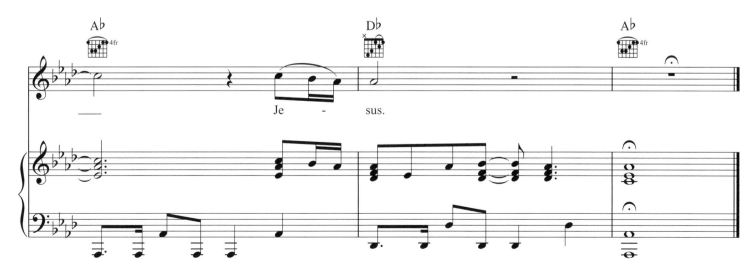

___ Je - sus.

JESUS LOVES ME

Words and Music by REUBEN MORGAN,
CHRIS TOMLIN and BEN GLOVER

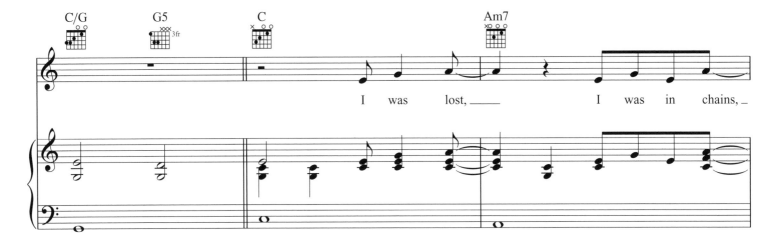

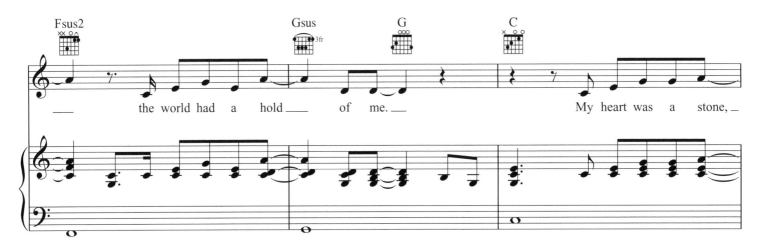

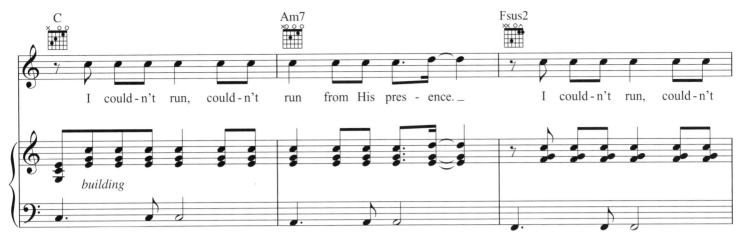

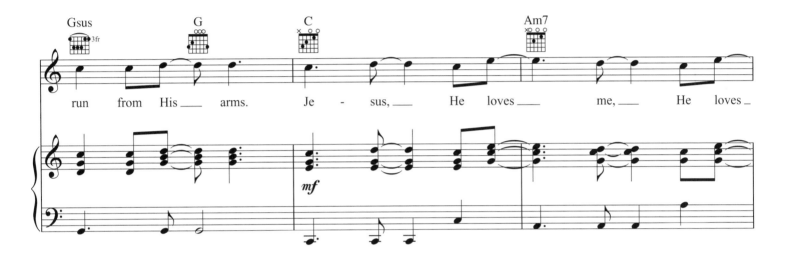

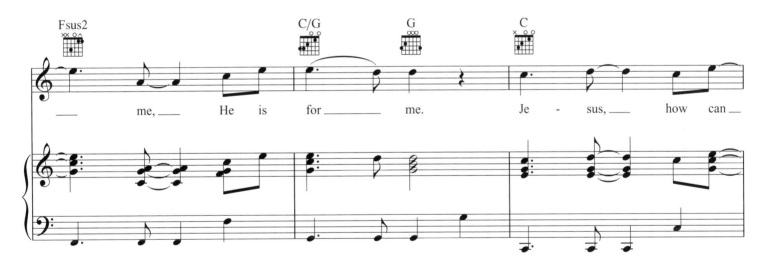

It was a fire ___ deep in my soul. ___ I'll nev-er be ___

___ the same. ___ I stepped out of the dark ___ and in-to the light ___

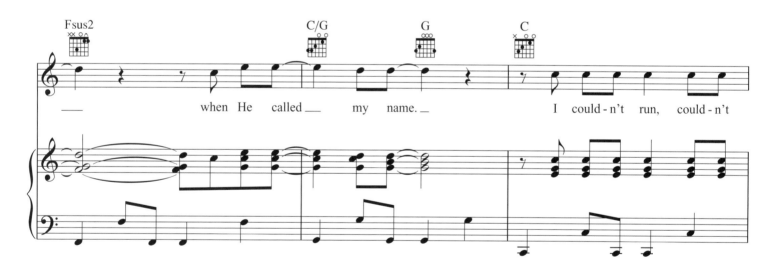

___ when He called ___ my name. ___ I could-n't run, could-n't

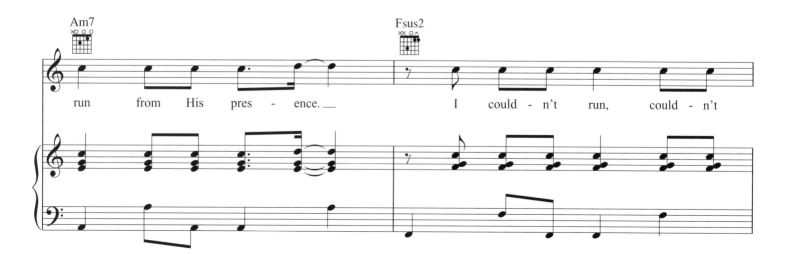

run from His pres - ence. ___ I could-n't run, could-n't

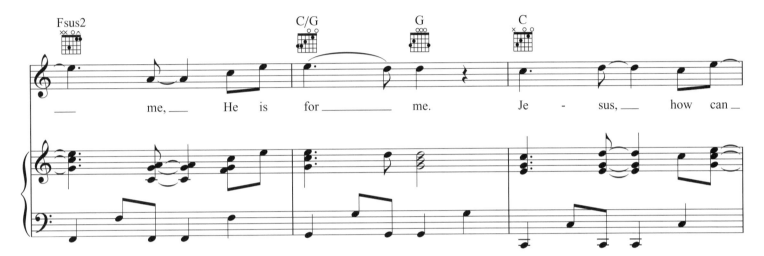

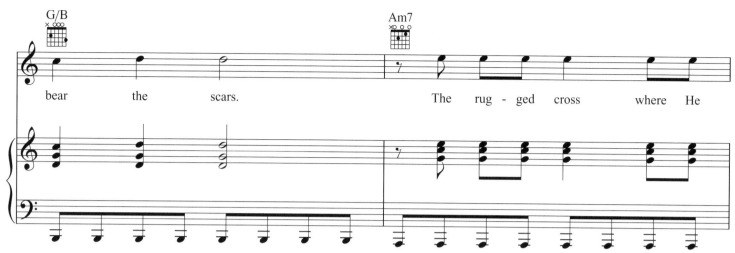

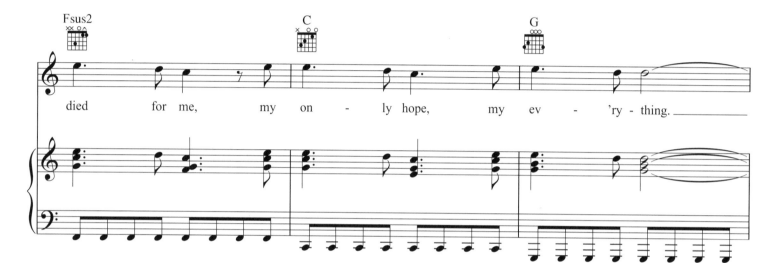

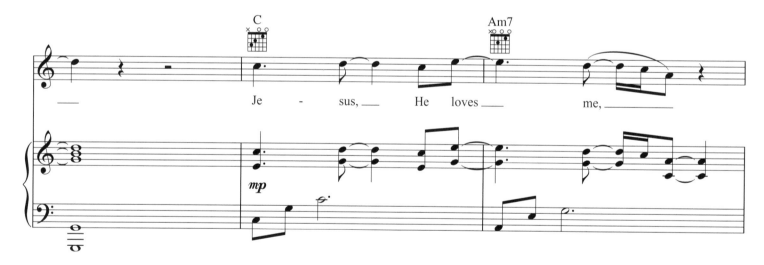

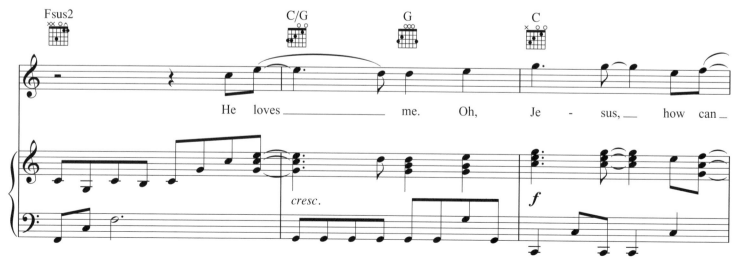

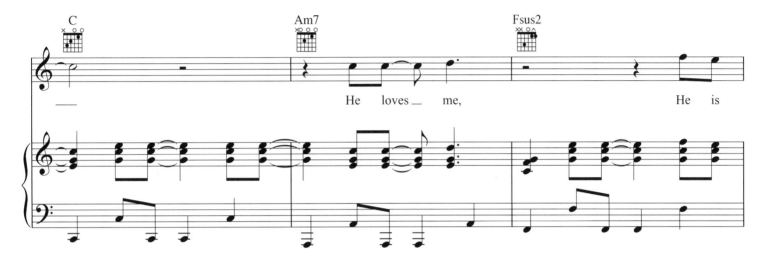

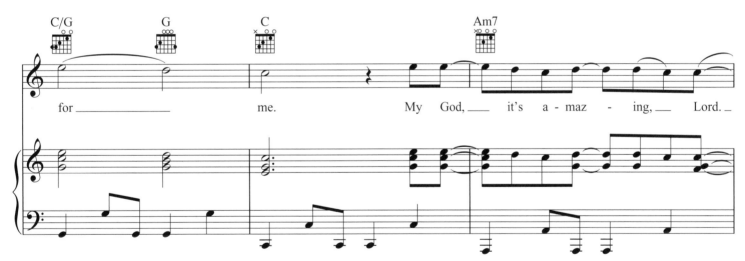

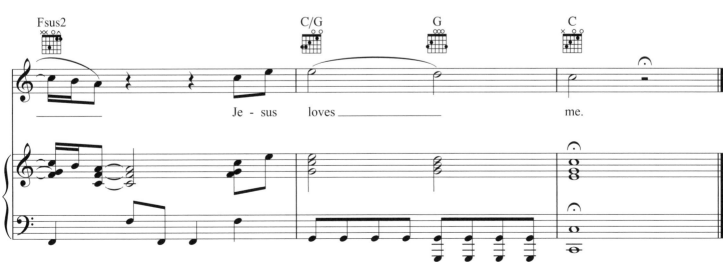

BOUNDARY LINES

Words and Music by CHRIS TOMLIN,
ED CASH and SCOTT CASH

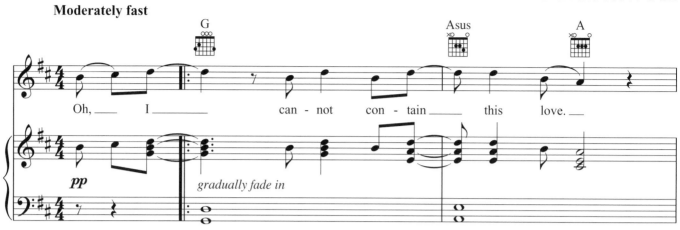

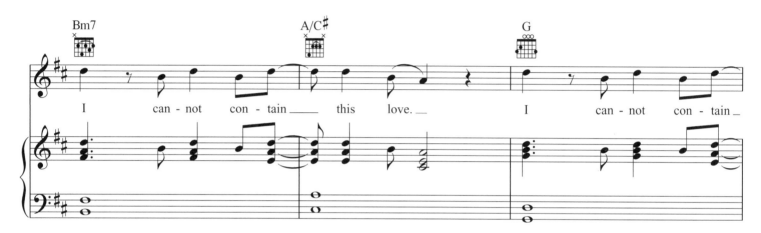

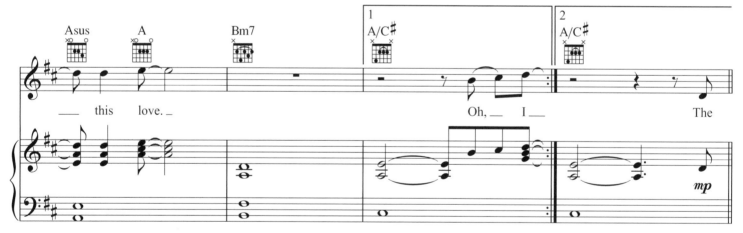

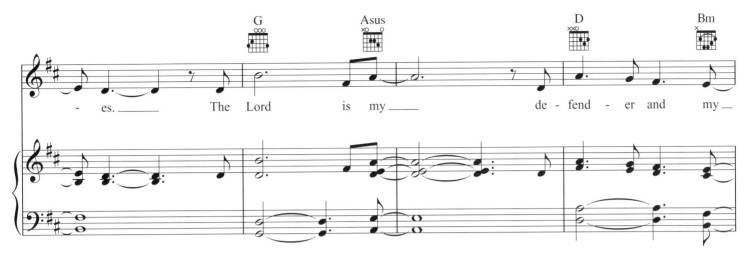

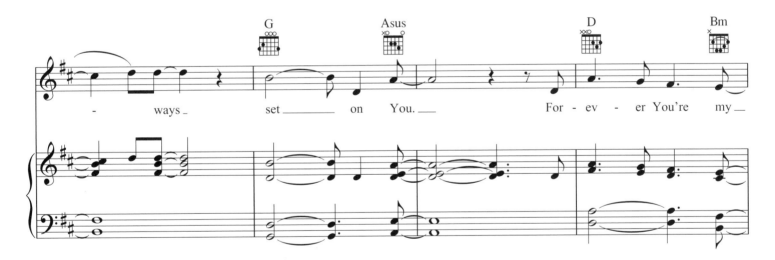

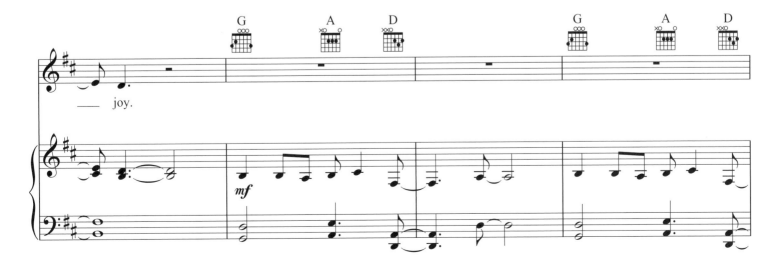

32

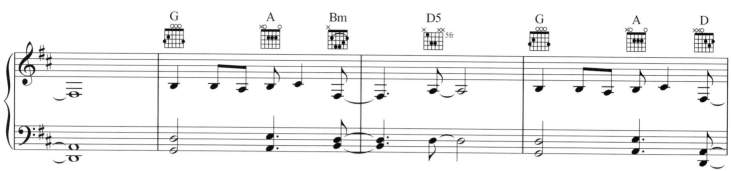

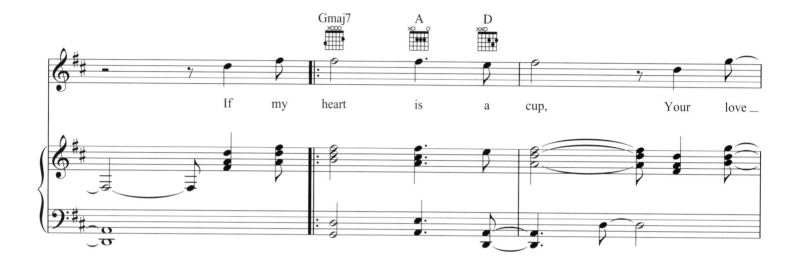

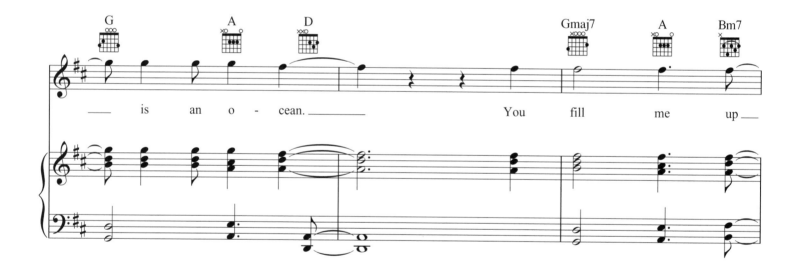

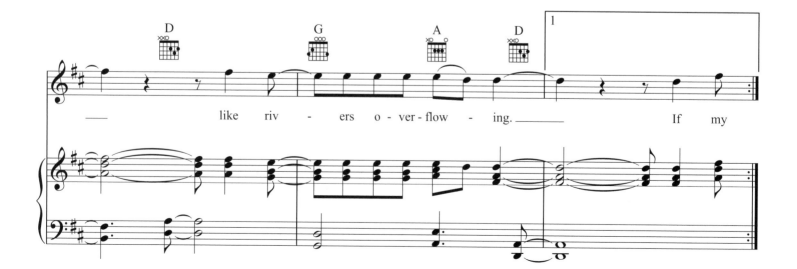

Sing cues 2nd time

(Oh, _____ oh, _____

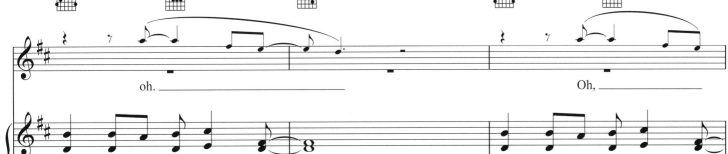

oh. _____ Oh, _____

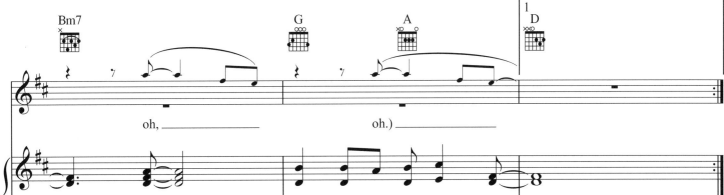

oh, _____ oh.) _____

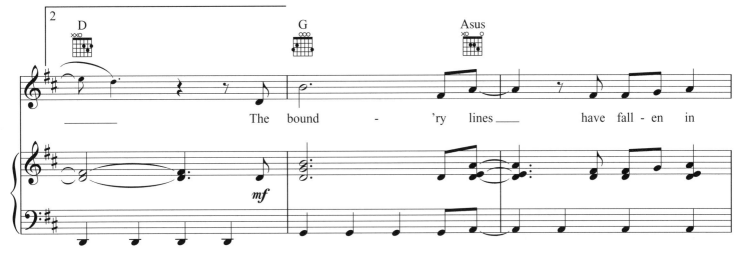

_____ The bound - 'ry lines _____ have fall - en in

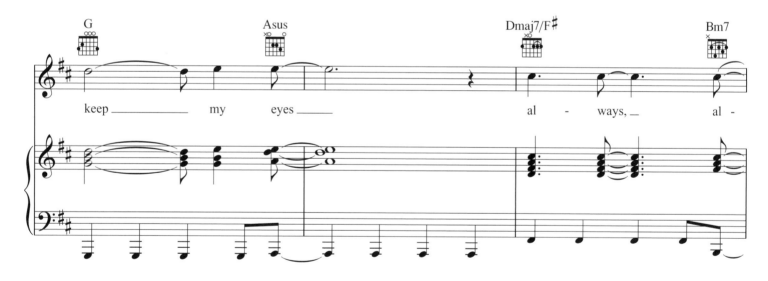

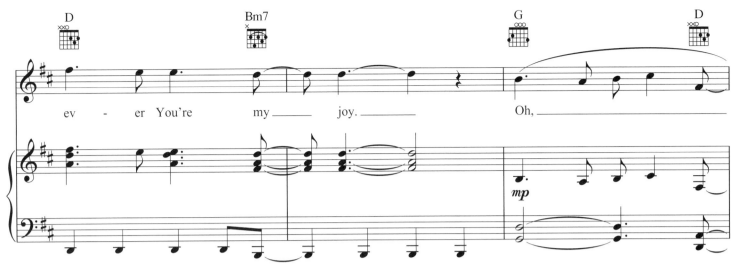

ev - er You're my ___ joy. ___ Oh, ___

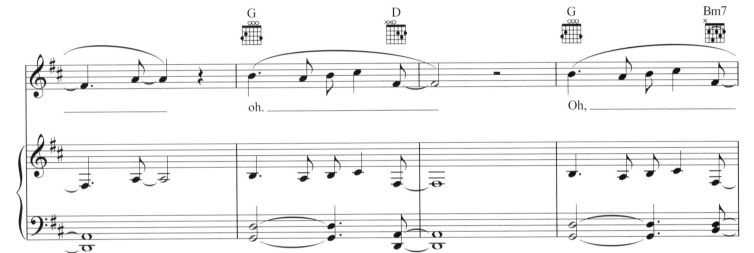

oh. ___ Oh, ___

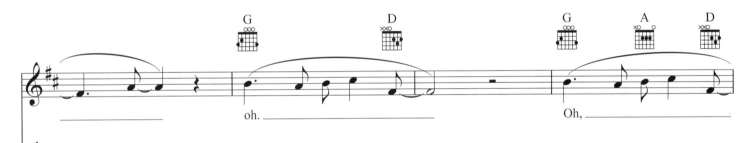

oh. ___ Oh, ___

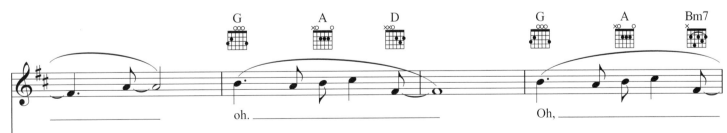

oh. ___ Oh, ___

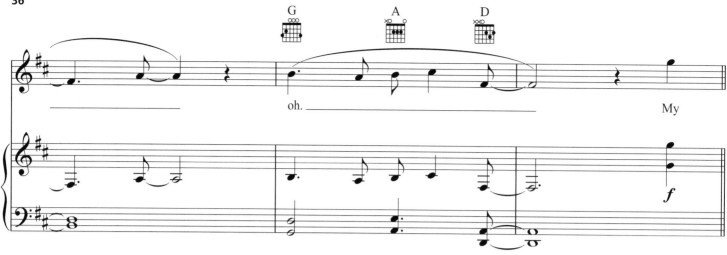

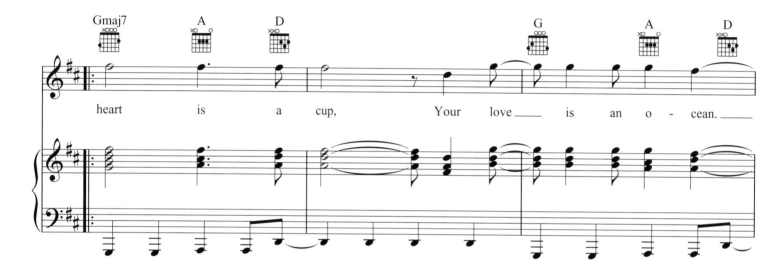

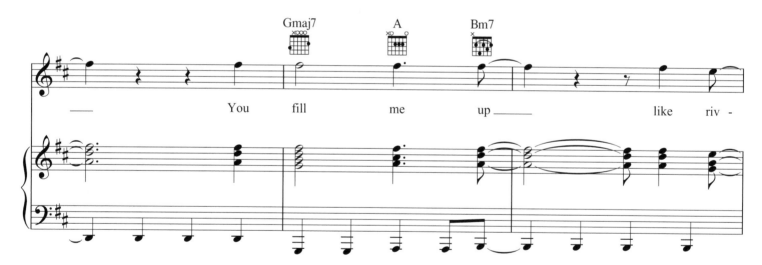

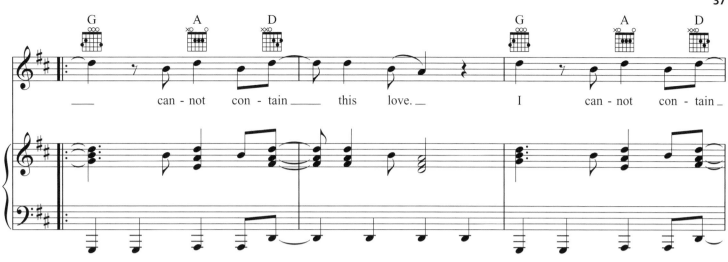

can - not con - tain___ this love.___ I can - not con - tain_

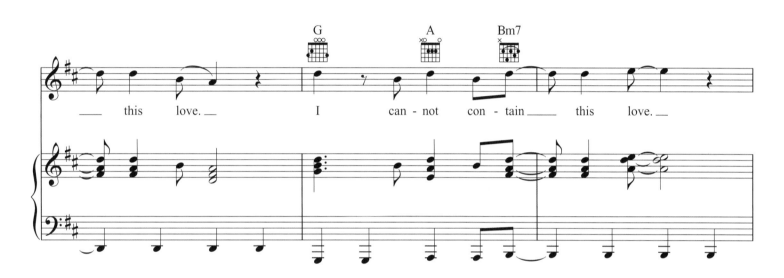

___ this love. ___ I can - not con - tain___ this love.___

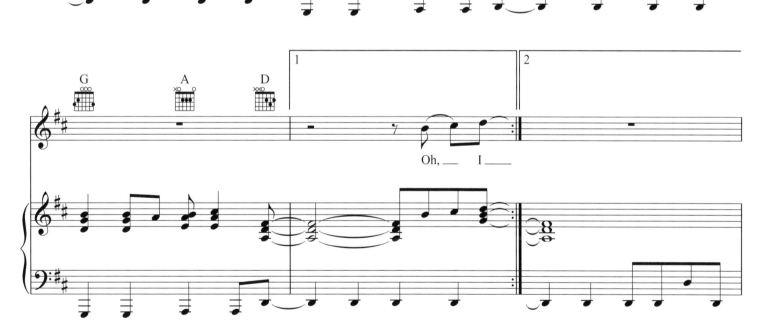

Oh, ___ I ___

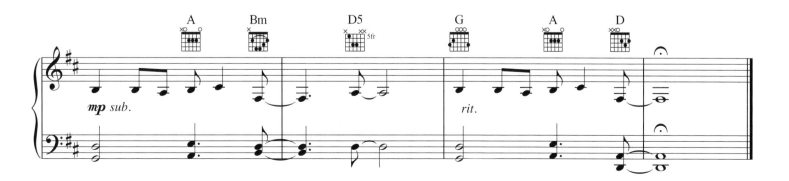

ALMIGHTY

Words and Music by CHRIS TOMLIN,
ED CASH and JARED ANDERSON

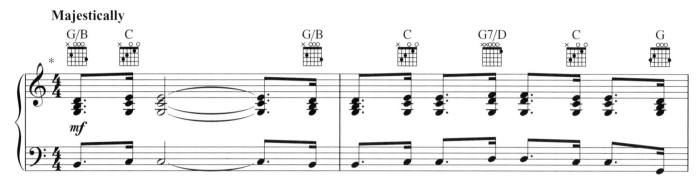

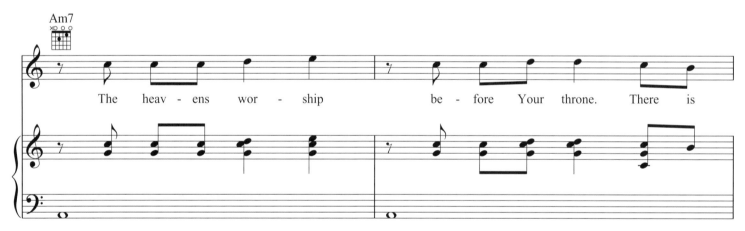

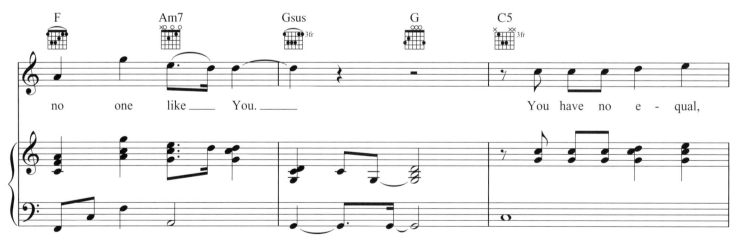

You have no ri - val, You stand a - lone.

The heav - ens wor - ship be - fore Your throne. There is no one like ____ You. ____ You have no e - qual,

* Recorded a half step lower.

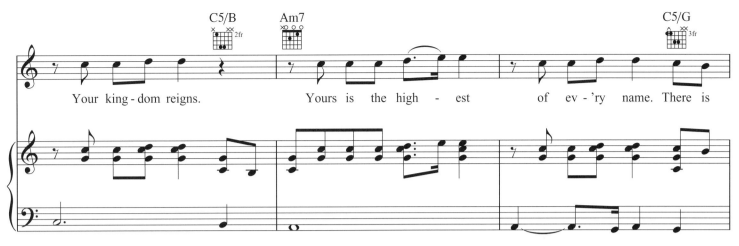

Your king-dom reigns. Yours is the high-est of ev-'ry name. There is

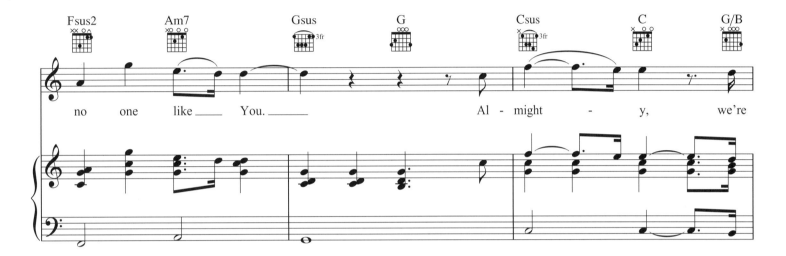

no one like ____ You. ____ Al-might-y, we're

stand-ing in the pres-ence of Your maj-es-ty. You're ho-ly.

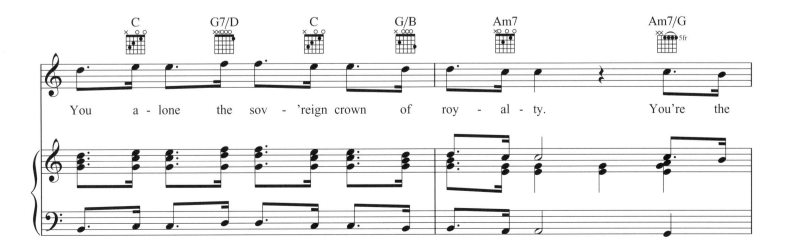

You a-lone the sov-'reign crown of roy-al-ty. You're the

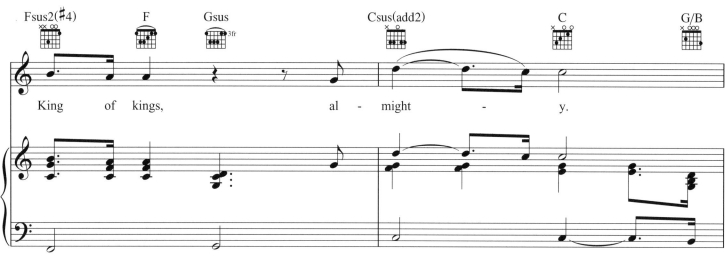

King of kings, al - might - y.

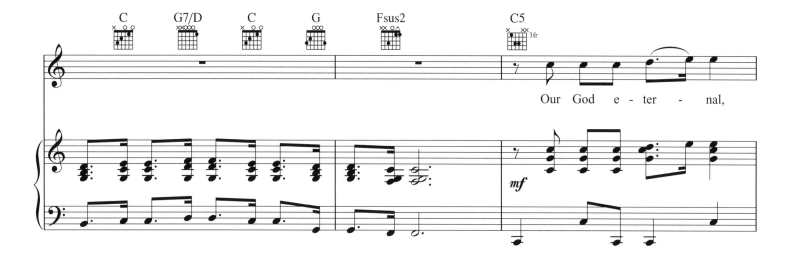

Our God e - ter - nal,

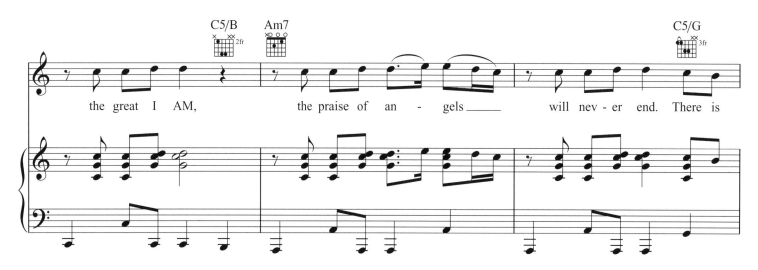

the great I AM, the praise of an - gels____ will nev - er end. There is

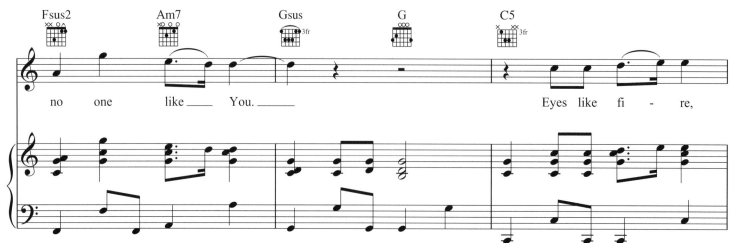

no one like ____ You. ____ Eyes like fi - re,

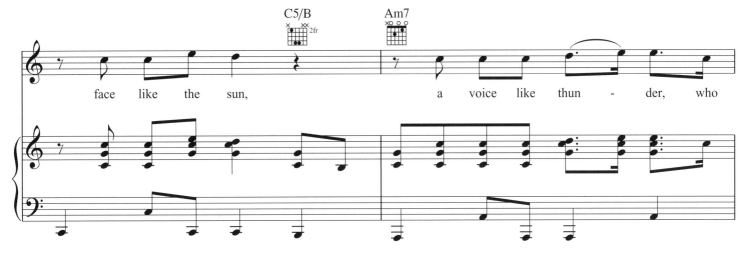

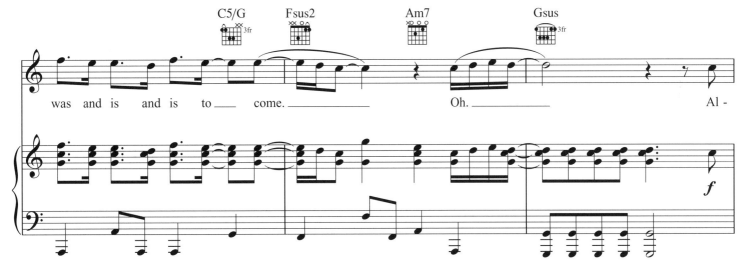

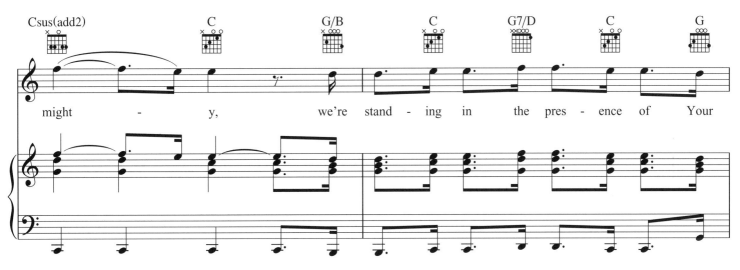

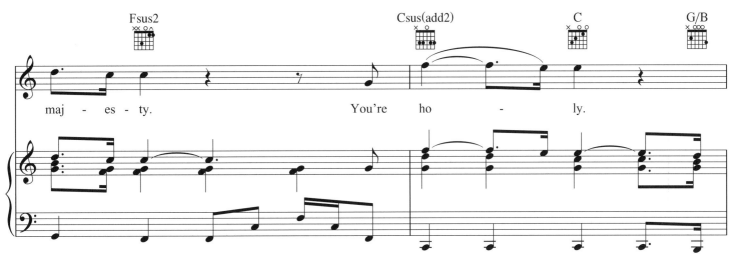

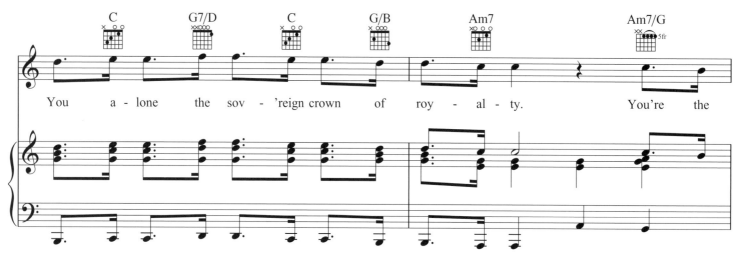

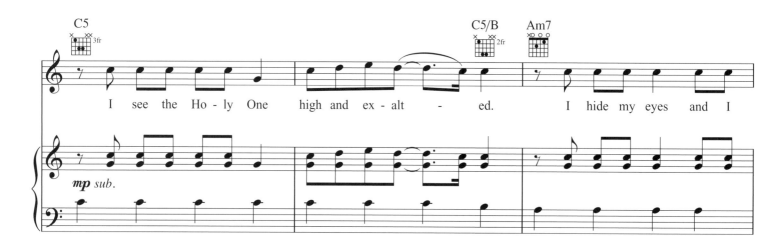

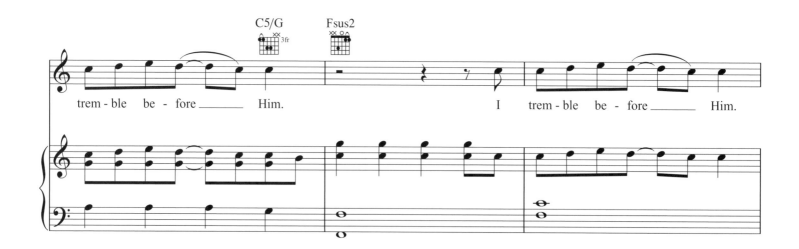

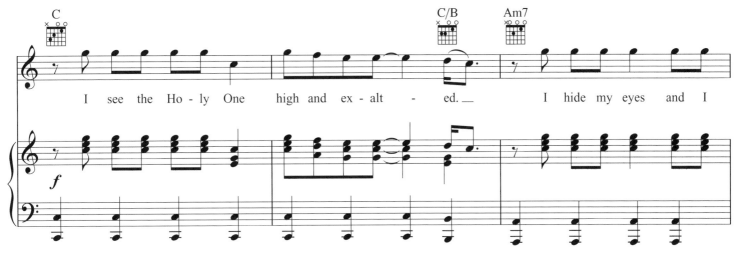

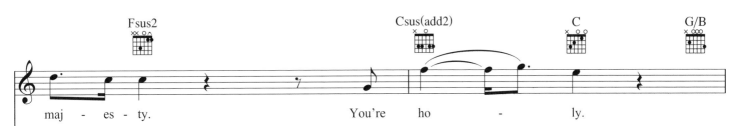

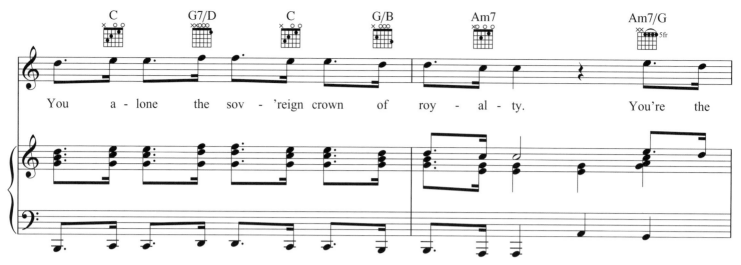

You a - lone the sov - 'reign crown of roy - al - ty. You're the

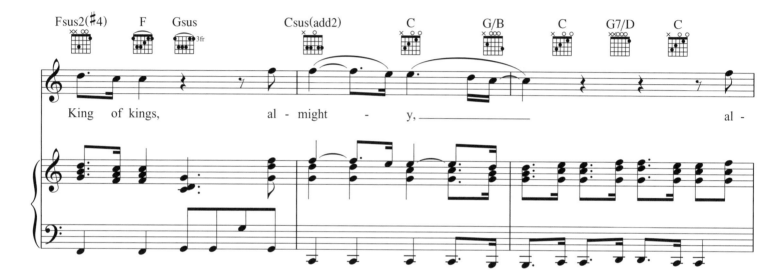

King of kings, al - might - y, _____ al -

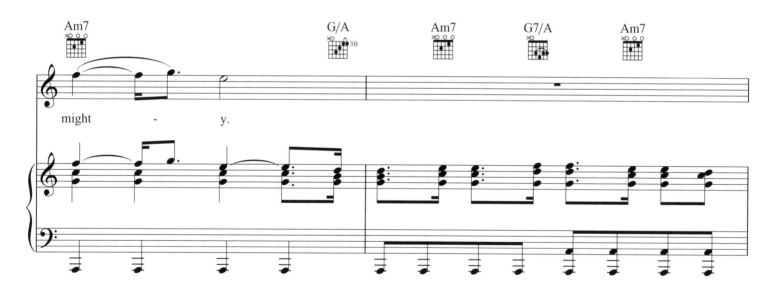

might - y.

THE ROAR

Words and Music by CHRIS TOMLIN,
ED CASH and WAYNE JOLLEY

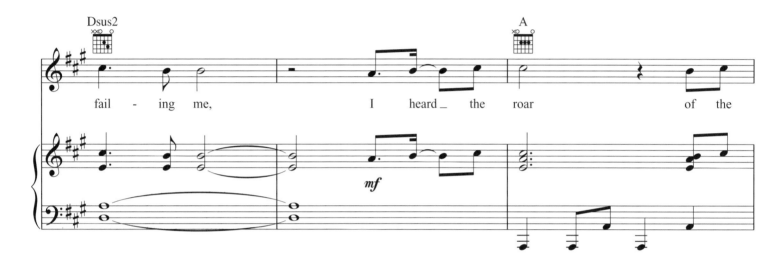

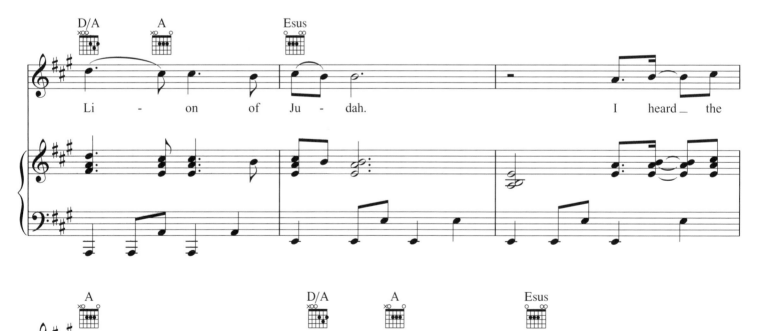

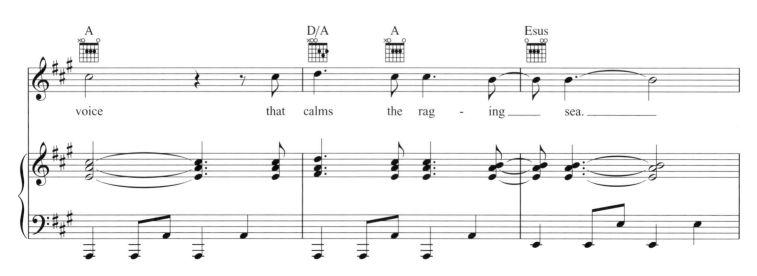

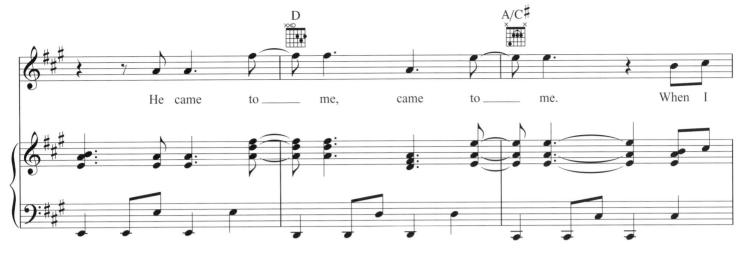

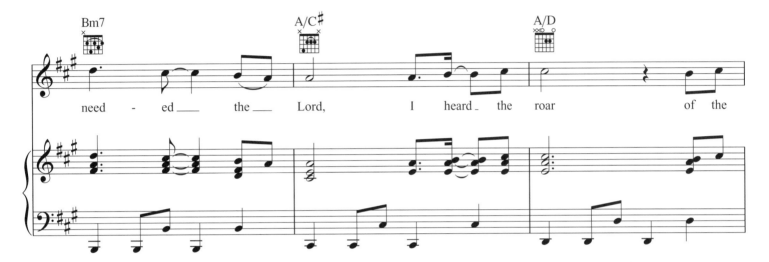

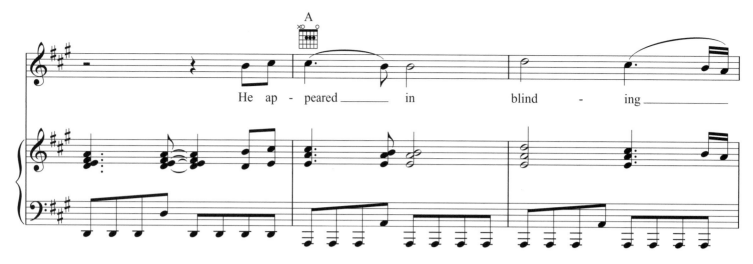

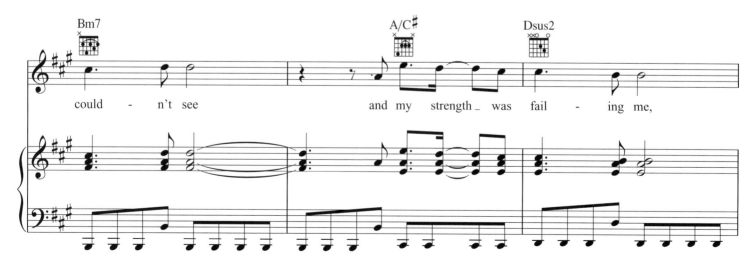

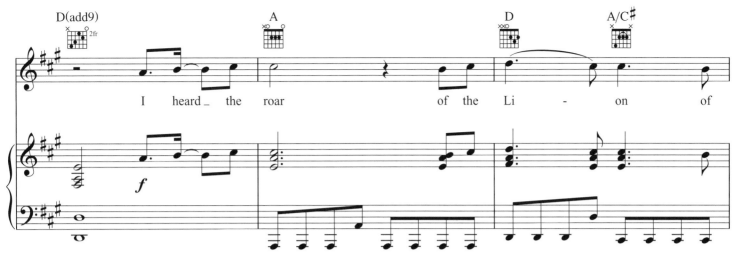

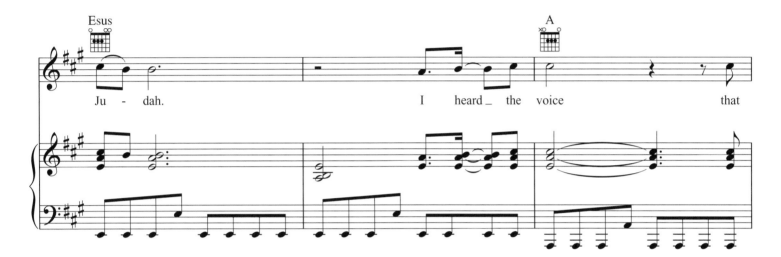

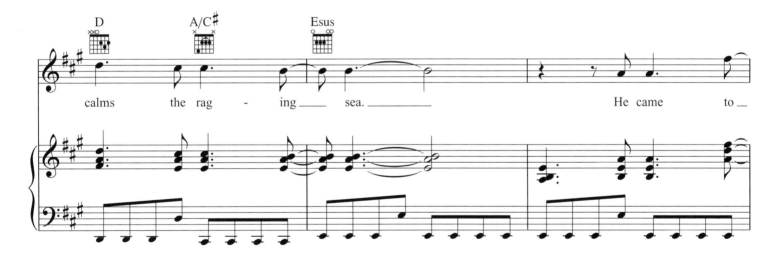

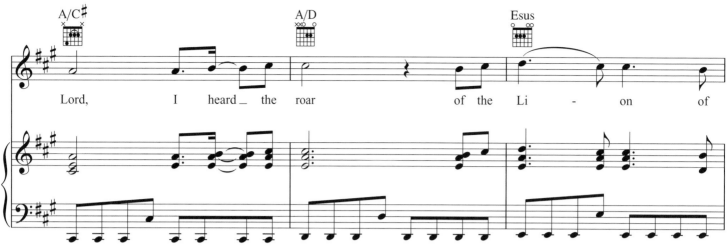

Lord, I heard the roar of the Li - on of

Ju - dah. When I lift - ed my hands, _

half-time feel

_ He lift - ed me up. _ All praise _ to the Sav -

- ior, all wor - ship to _ God. _ And with all _

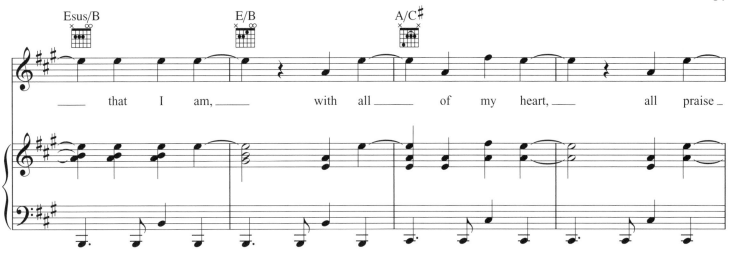

that I am, _____ with all _____ of my heart, _____ all praise _

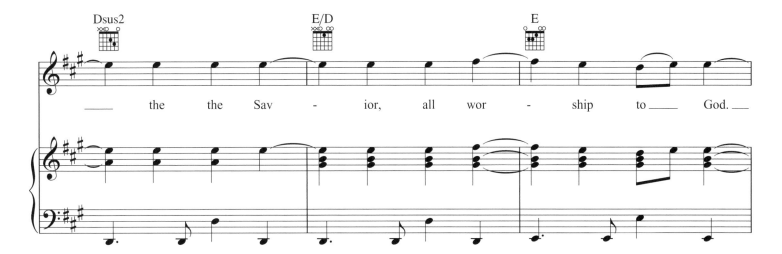

_____ the the Sav - ior, all wor - ship to _____ God. _

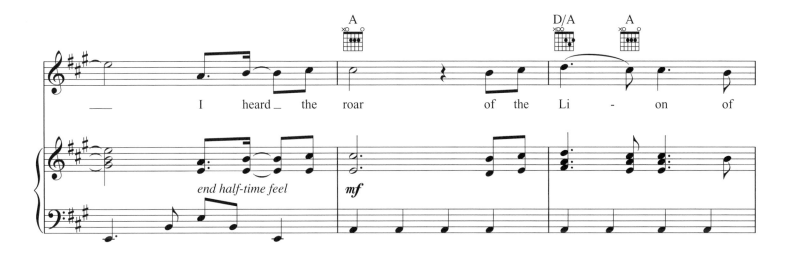

_____ I heard _ the roar of the Li - on of

end half-time feel *mf*

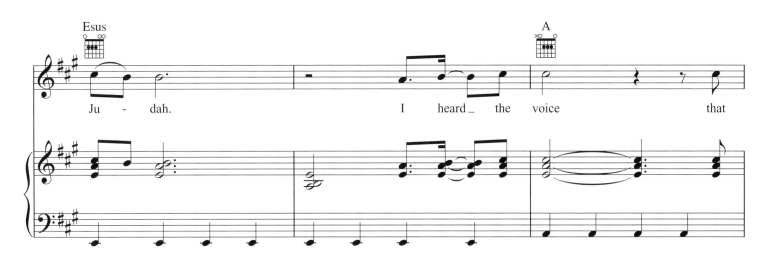

Ju - dah. I heard _ the voice that

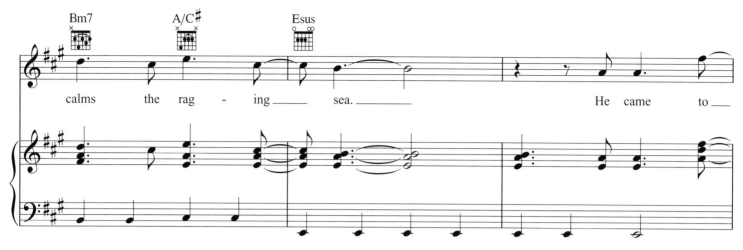

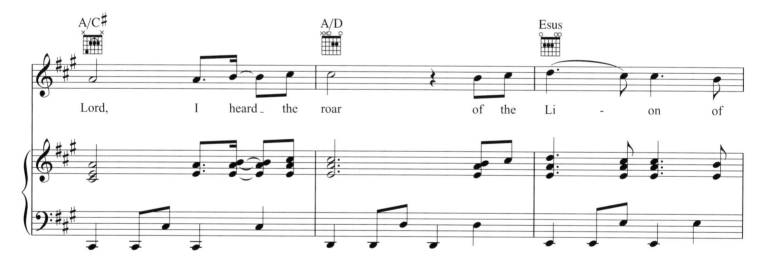

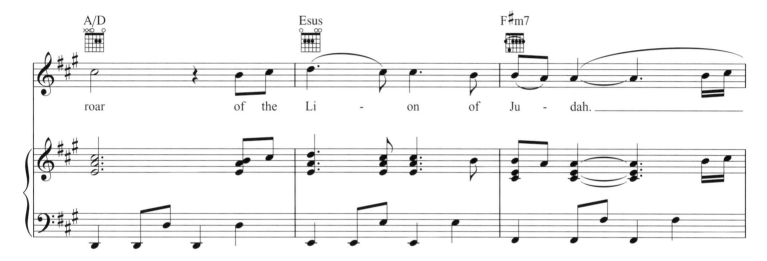

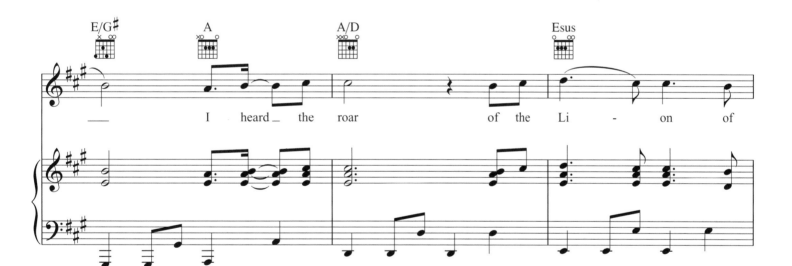

FEAR NOT

Words and Music by CHRIS TOMLIN
and ED CASH

Strong Rock beat

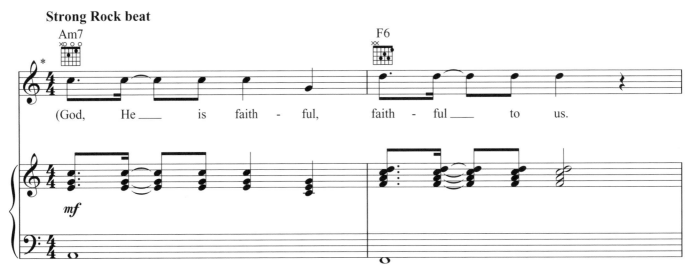

(God, He ___ is faith - ful, faith - ful ___ to us.

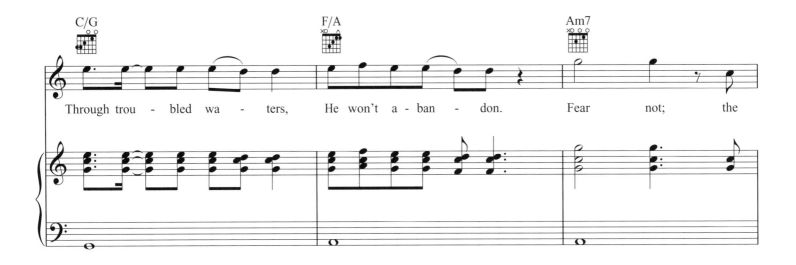

Through trou - bled wa - ters, He won't a - ban - don. Fear not; the

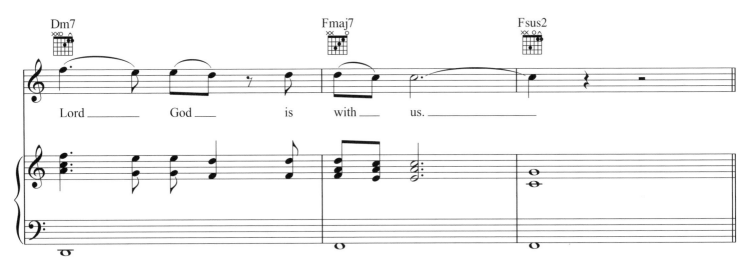

Lord ___ God ___ is with ___ us. ___

* *Recorded a half step lower.*

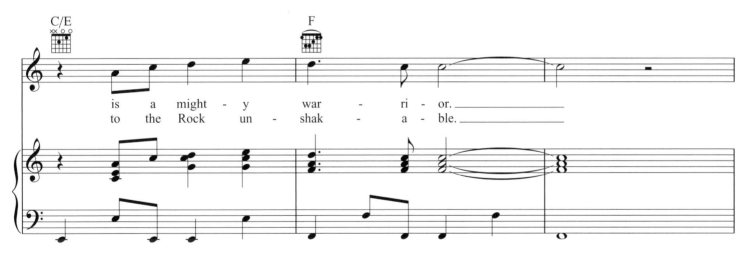

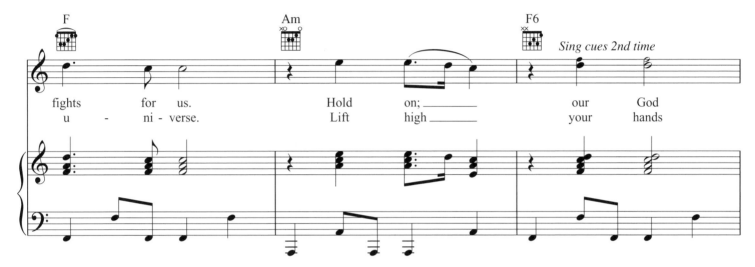

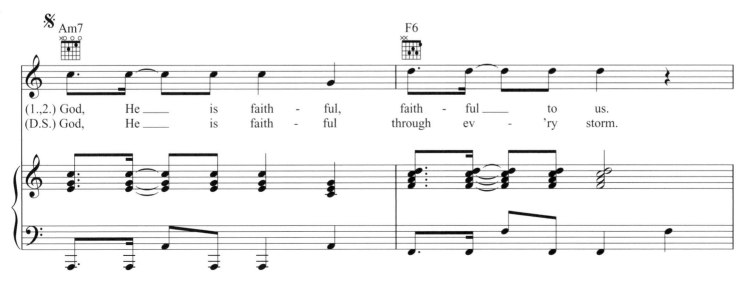

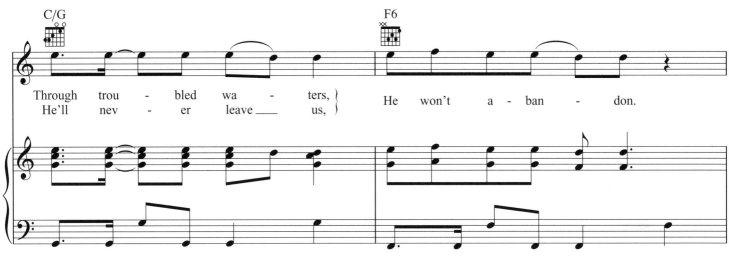

Through trou - bled wa - ters,
He'll nev - er leave us,
He won't a - ban - don.

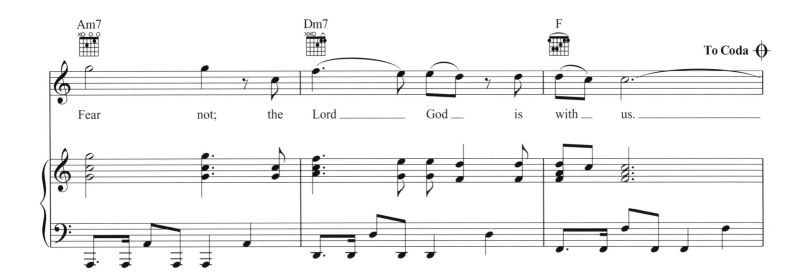

Fear not; the Lord God is with us.

To Coda ⊕

D.S. al Coda

CODA ⊕

truth is ___ a sword, the bat - tle is ___ the Lord's. Sure - ly, He will de - liv -

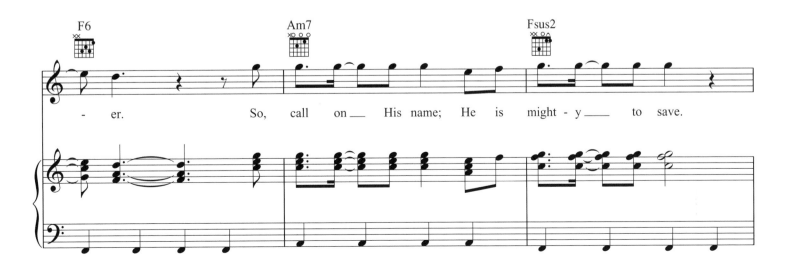

- er. So, call on ___ His name; He is might - y ___ to save.

Sure - ly, He will de - liv - er. The truth is ___ a sword, the

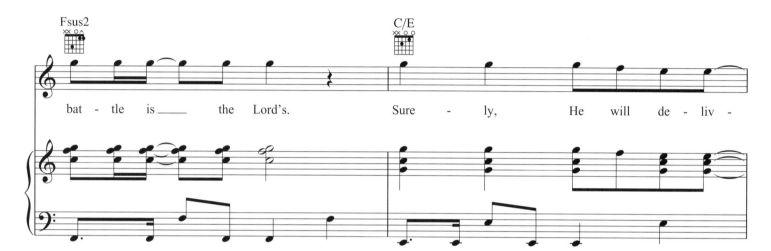

bat - tle is ___ the Lord's. Sure - ly, He will de - liv -

- er. So, call on ___ His name; He is

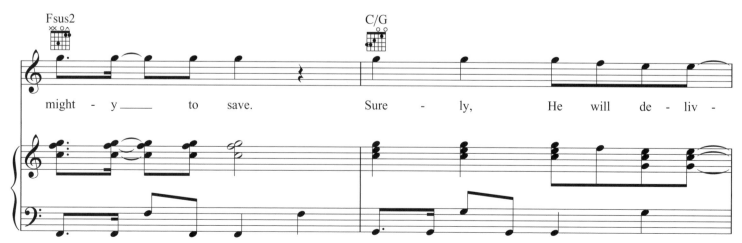

might - y ___ to save. Sure - ly, He will de - liv -

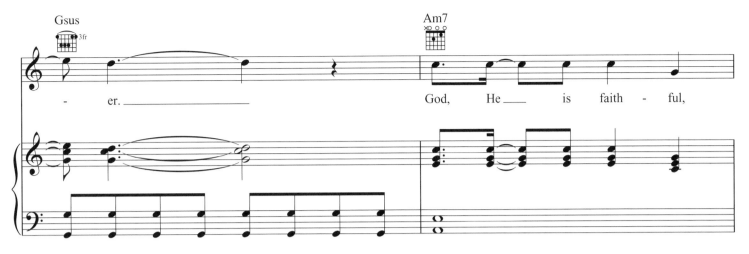

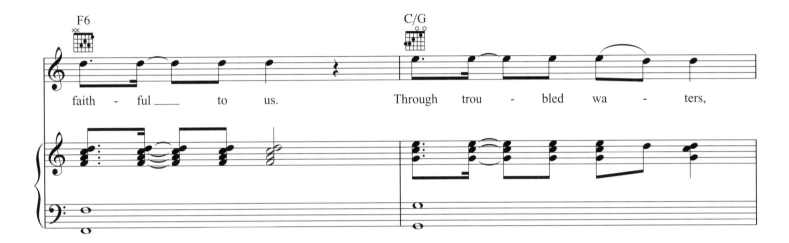

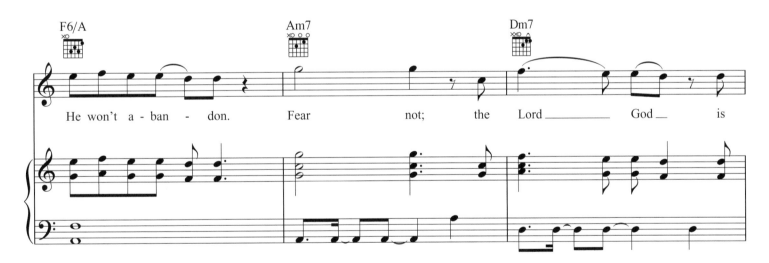

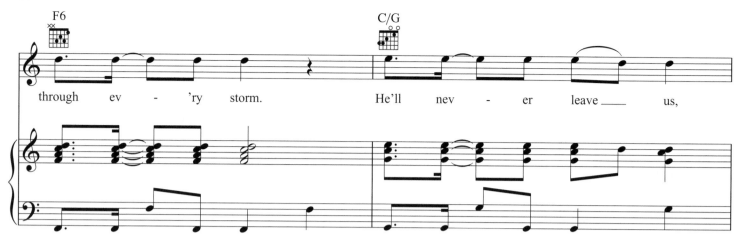

through ev - 'ry storm. He'll nev - er leave ___ us,

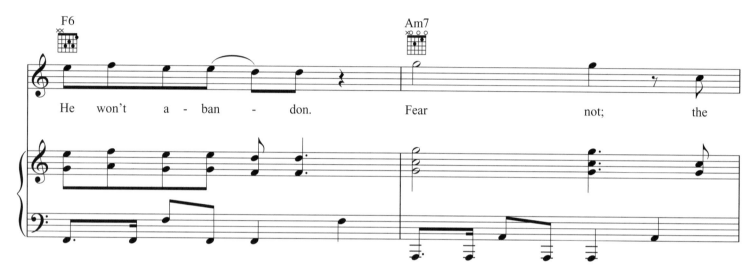

He won't a - ban - don. Fear not; the

Lord ___ God ___ is with ___ us.
Fear not; the Lord ___ God ___ is

with ___ us.

THE TABLE

Words and Music by CHRIS TOMLIN,
ED CASH and WAYNE JOLLEY

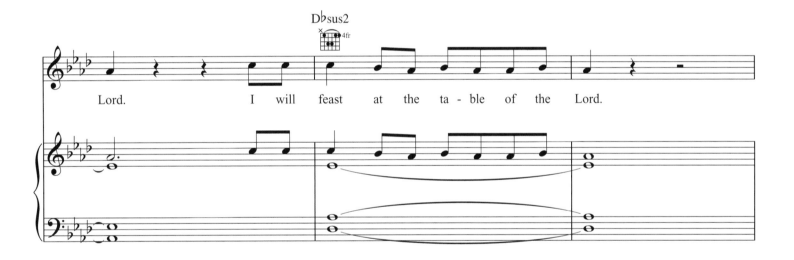

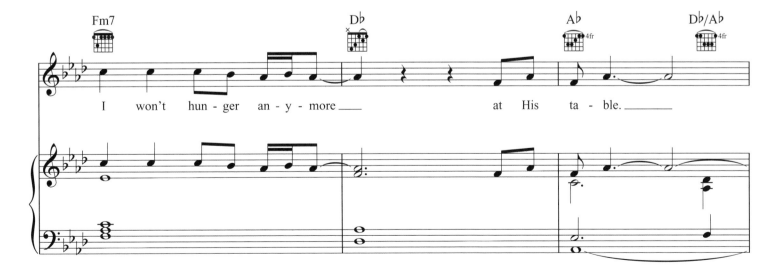

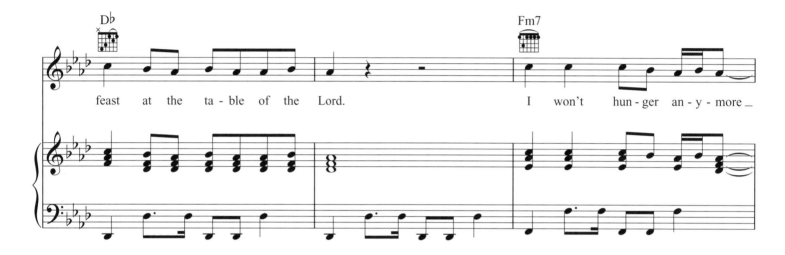

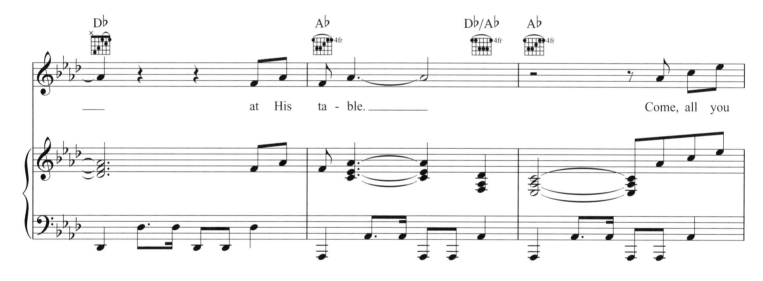

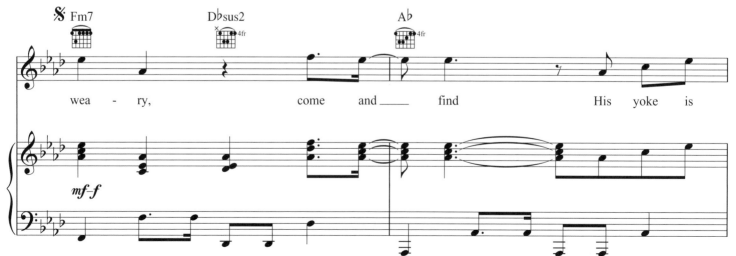

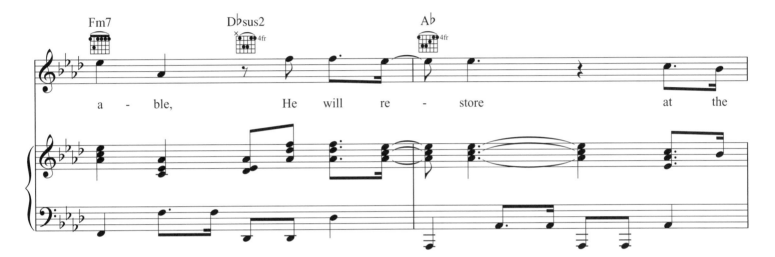

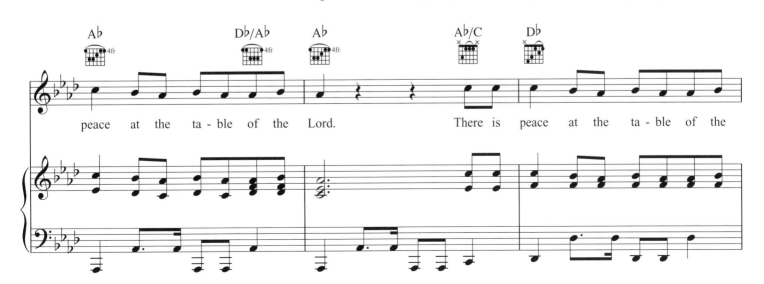

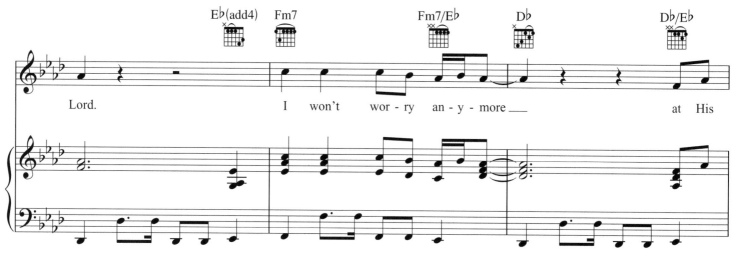

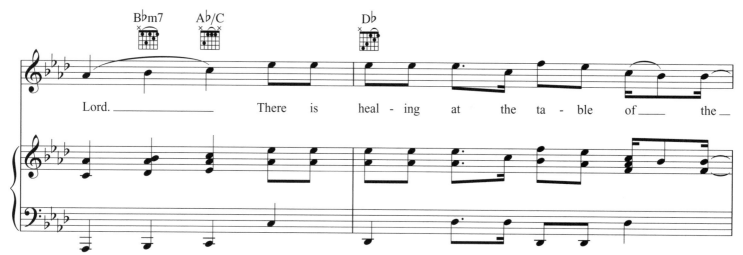

D.S. al Coda

wea - ry, come and __ find His yoke is eas - y, His bur - den __

__ light. He is a - ble, He will re -

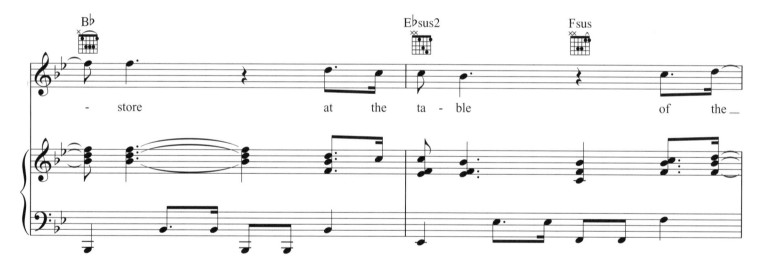

- store at the ta - ble of the __

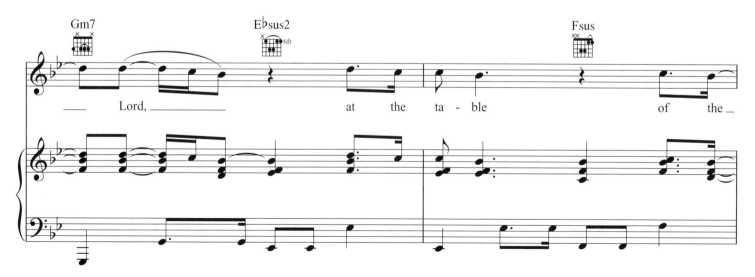

__ Lord, __ at the ta - ble of the __

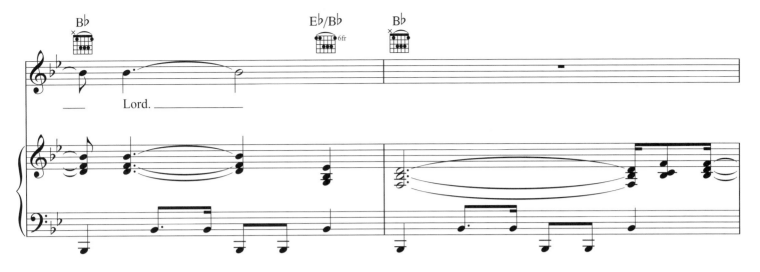

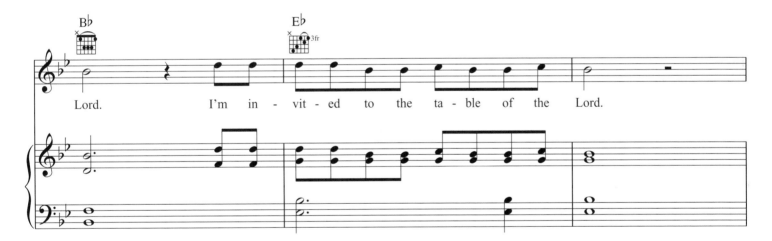

PSALM 100

Words and Music by JASON INGRAM
and CHRIS TOMLIN

With energy

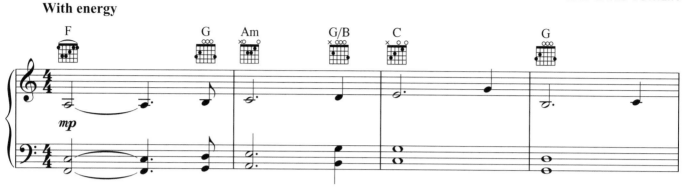

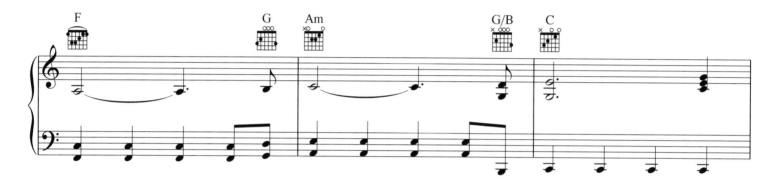

En - ter ___ in ___

through the ___ gates. ___
to His ___ courts. ___

En - ter ___ in ___
En - ter ___ in ___

here with ___ praise. ___
with grate - ful ___ hearts. ___

Come be - fore _____ Him, come bring your

song. We are His ___ peo - ple,

He is our ___ God. _____

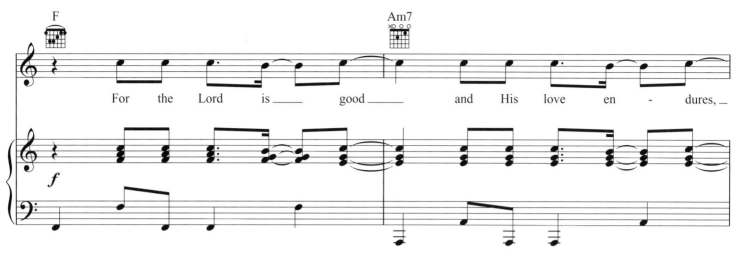

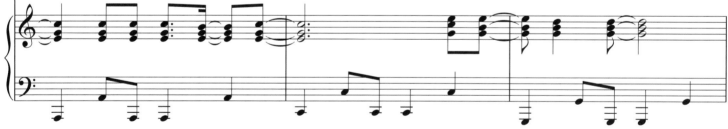

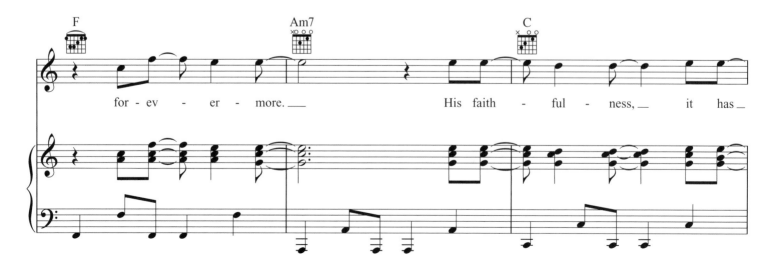

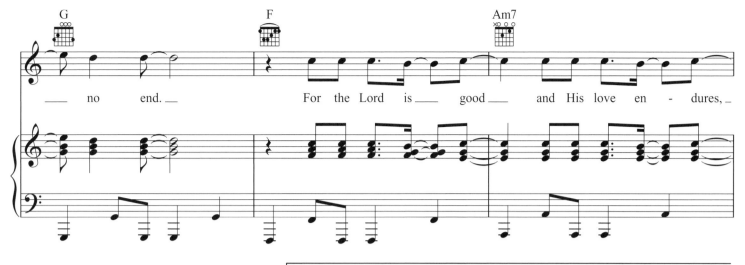

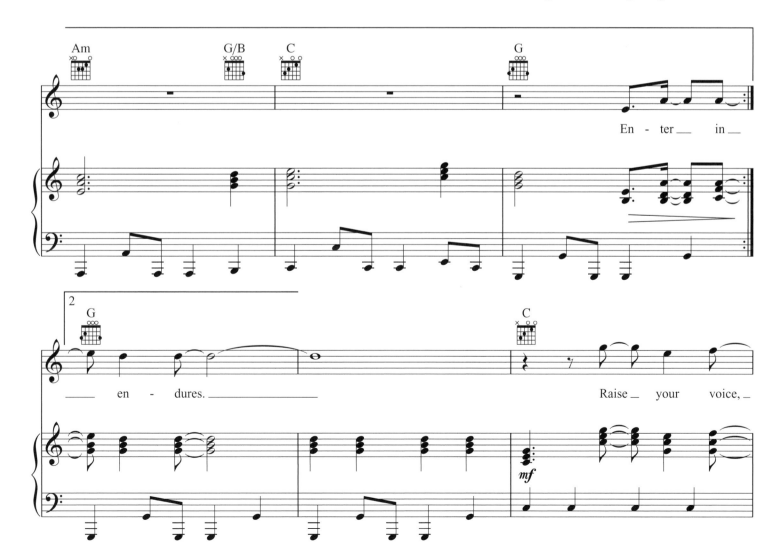

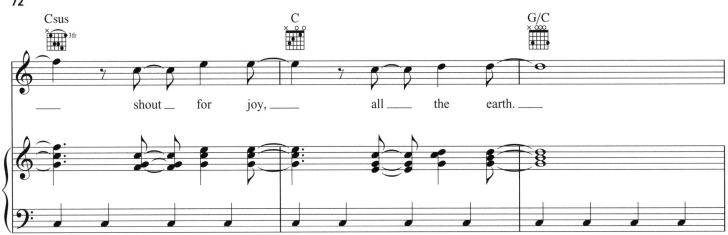

shout __ for joy, ___ all __ the earth. ___

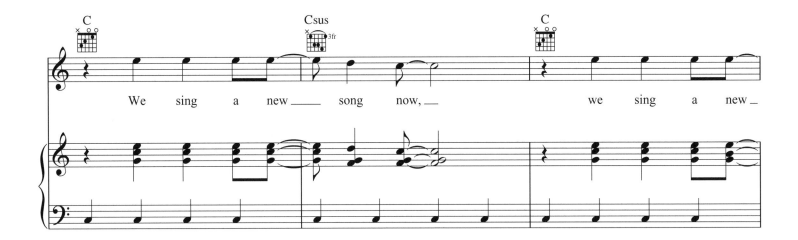

We sing a new ___ song now, ___ we sing a new _

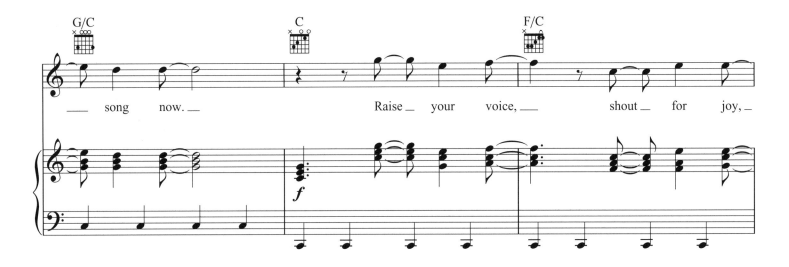

___ song now. ___ Raise __ your voice, ___ shout __ for joy, _

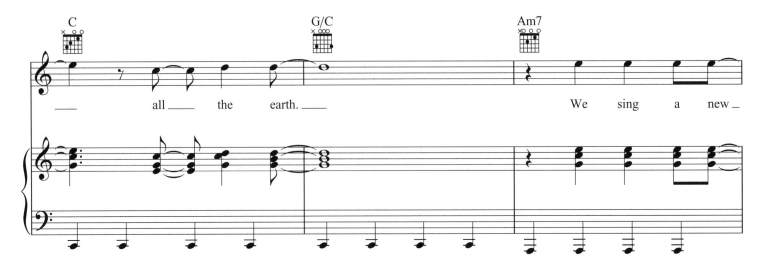

___ all __ the earth. ___ We sing a new _

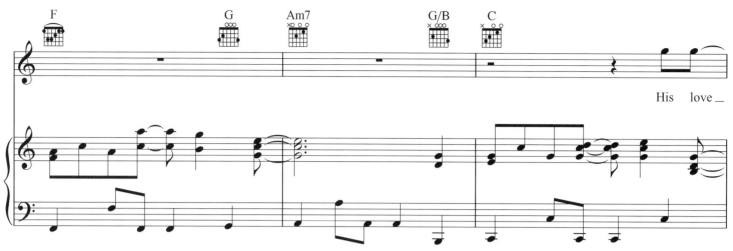

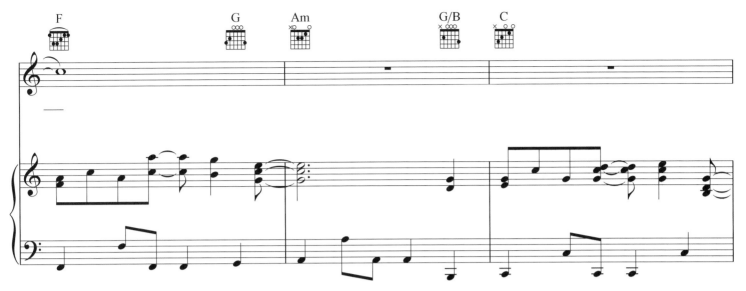

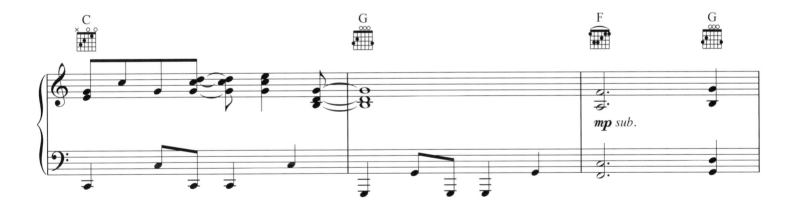

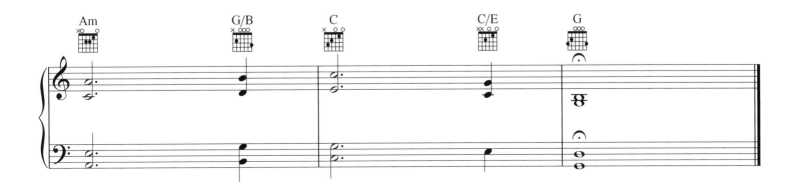

I WILL BOAST

Words and Music by JASON INGRAM
and CHRIS TOMLIN

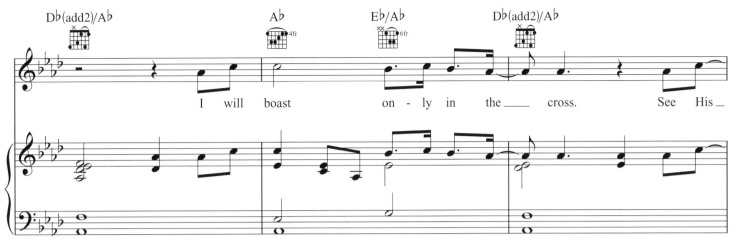

I will boast on-ly in the ___ cross. See His ___

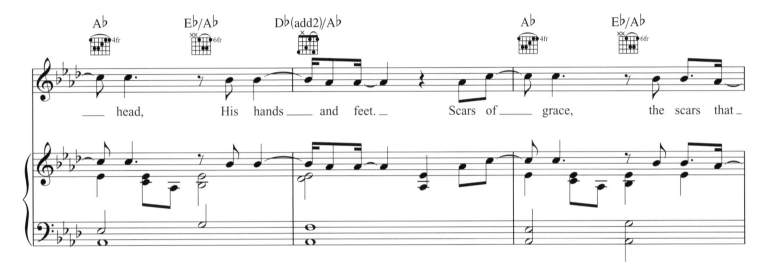

___ head, His hands ___ and feet. ___ Scars of ___ grace, the scars that ___

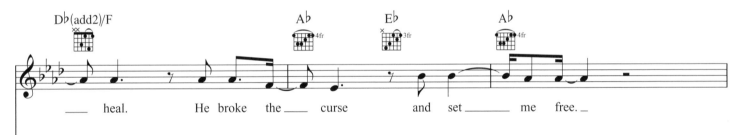

___ heal. He broke the ___ curse and set ___ me free. ___

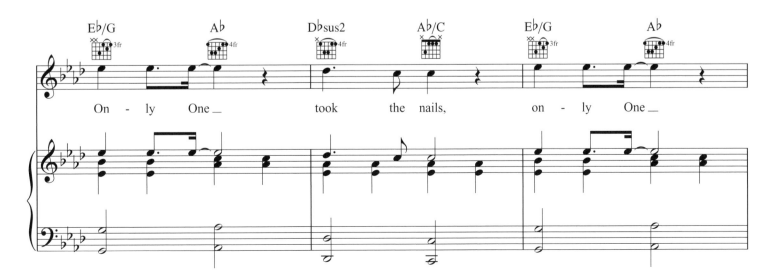

On-ly One ___ took the nails, on-ly One ___

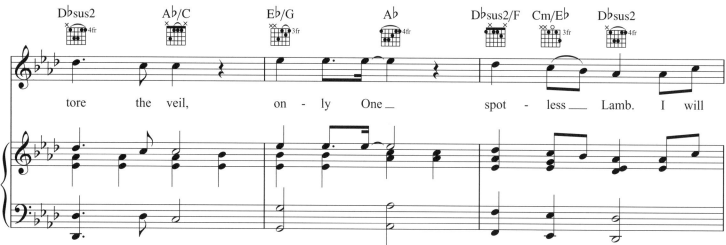

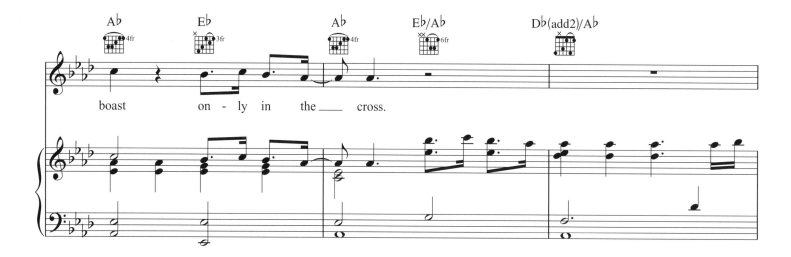

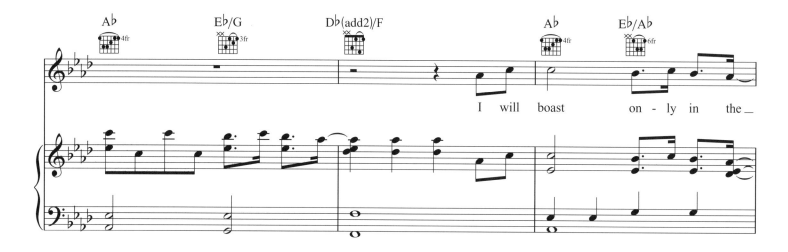

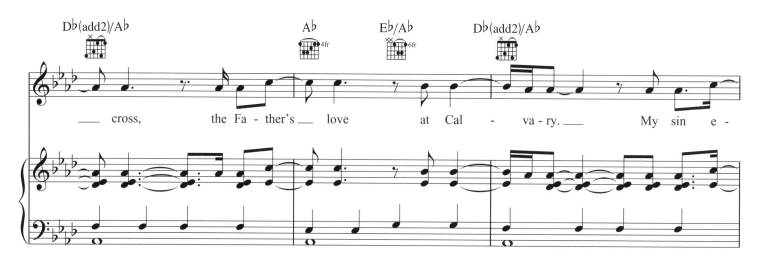

-rased; my debt, ___ He paid. ___ This is my ___ hope, the song I ___

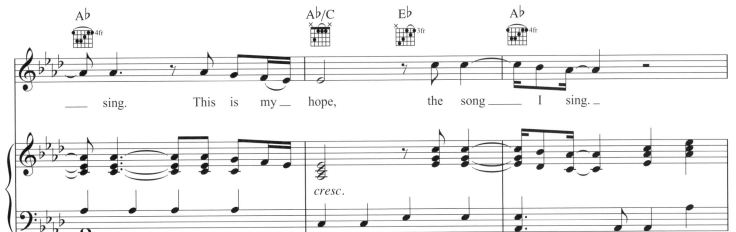

___ sing. This is my ___ hope, the song ___ I sing. ___

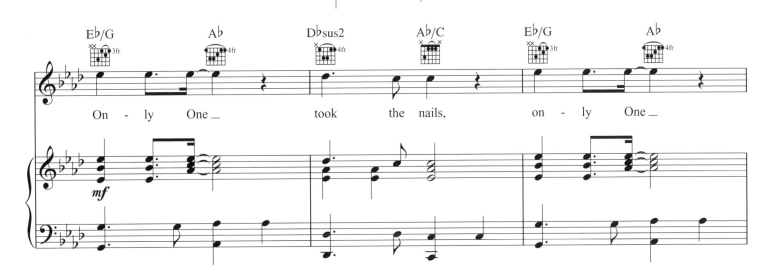

On - ly One ___ took the nails, on - ly One ___

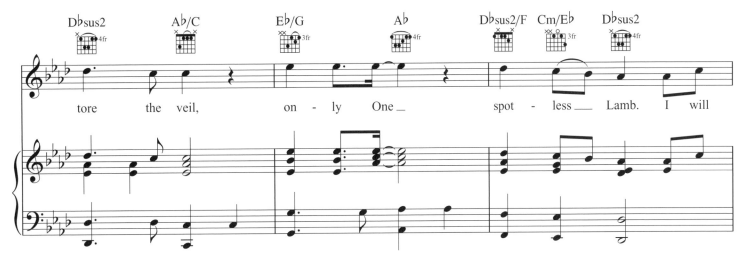

tore the veil, on - ly One ___ spot - less ___ Lamb. I will

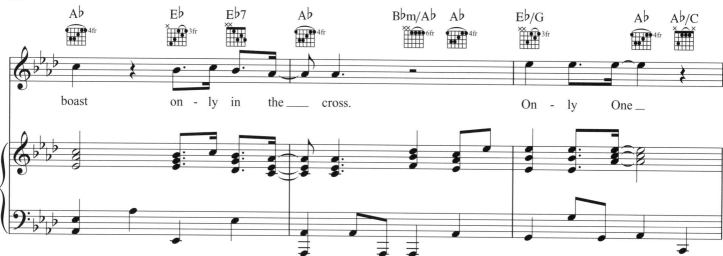

boast on - ly in the ___ cross. On - ly One ___

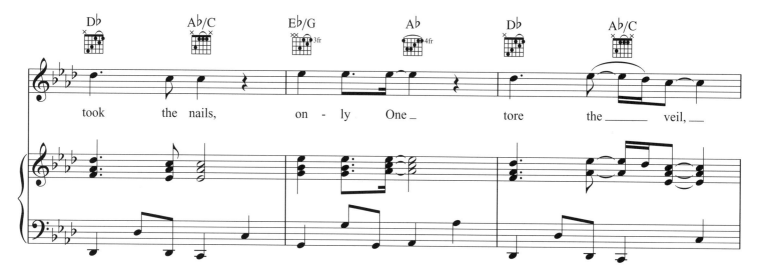

took the nails, on - ly One ___ tore the ___ veil, ___

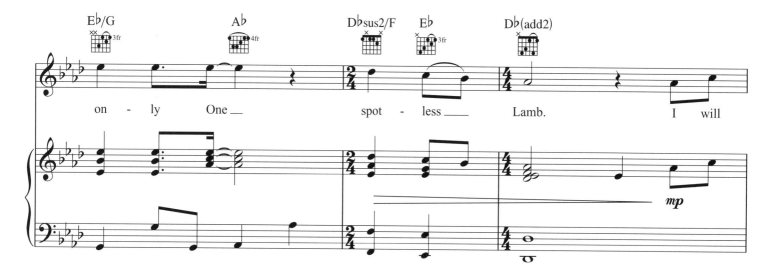

on - ly One ___ spot - less ___ Lamb. I will

boast on - ly in the ___ cross. I will boast on - ly in the ___

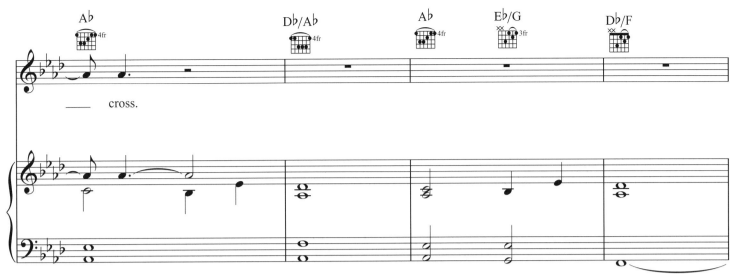

cross.

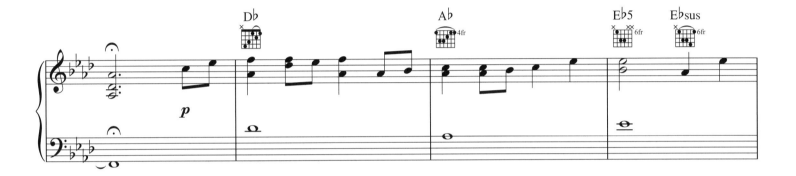

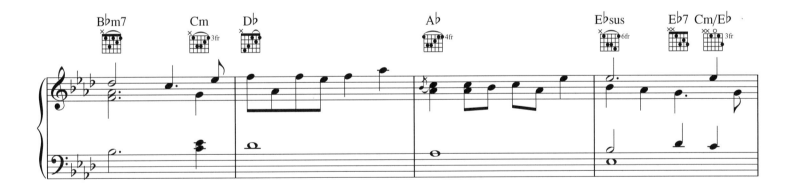

JESUS, THIS IS YOU

Words and Music by
JONAS MYRIN

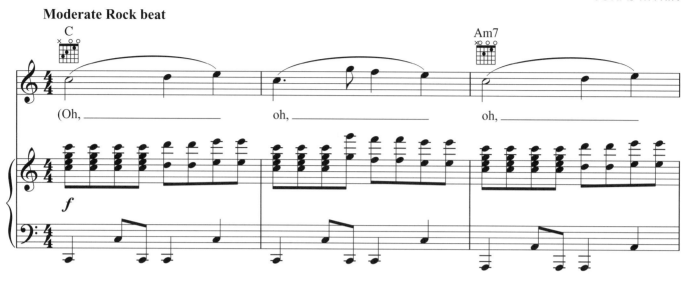

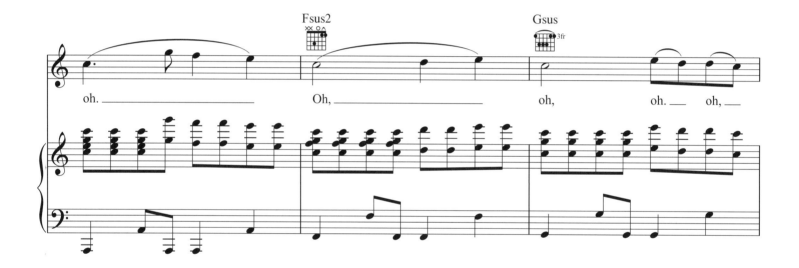

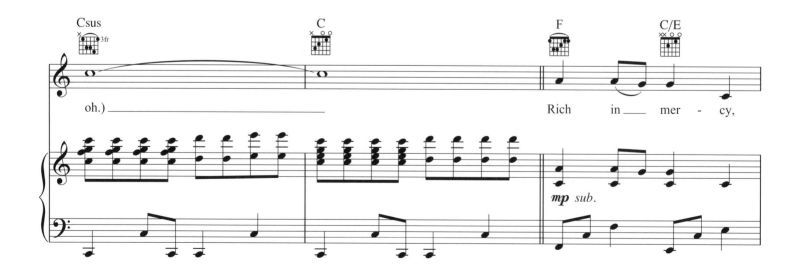

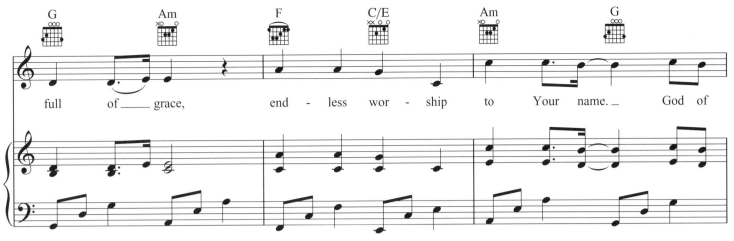

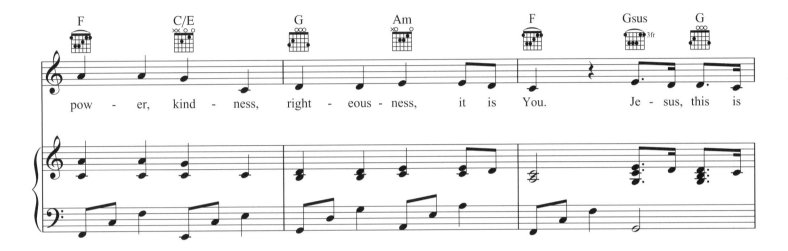

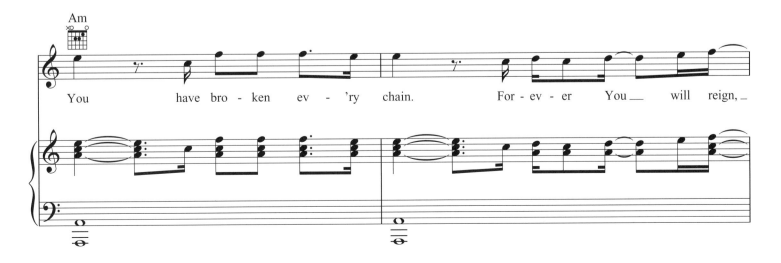

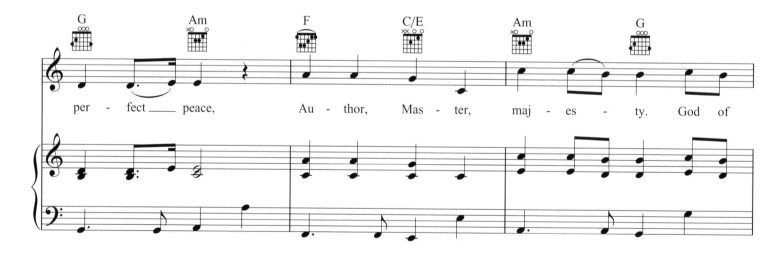

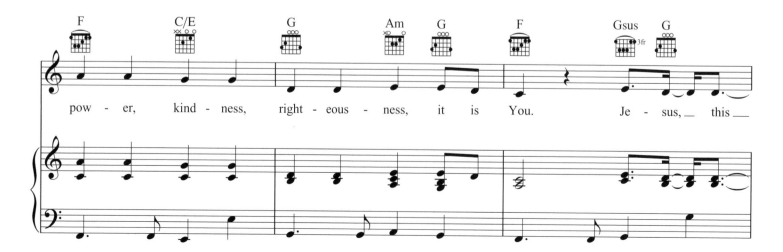

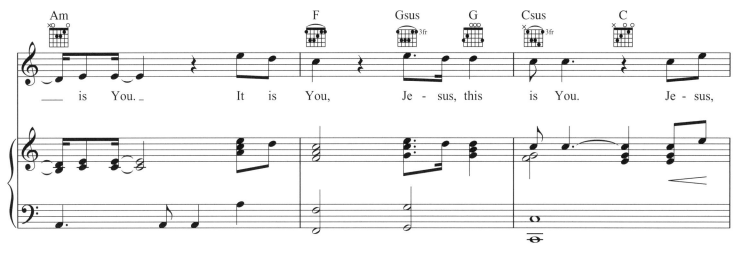

_ is You. _ It is You, Je - sus, this is You. Je - sus,

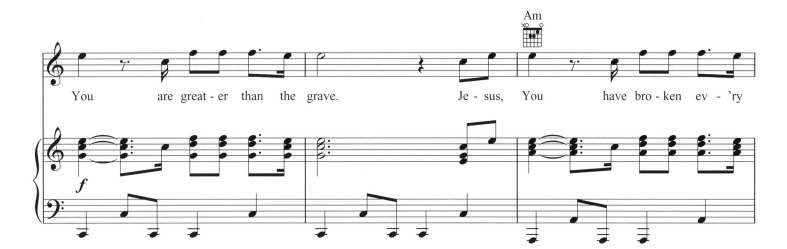

You are great - er than the grave. Je - sus, You have bro - ken ev - 'ry

chain. Fov - ev - er You _ will reign, _ for - ev - er we _ will sing. _

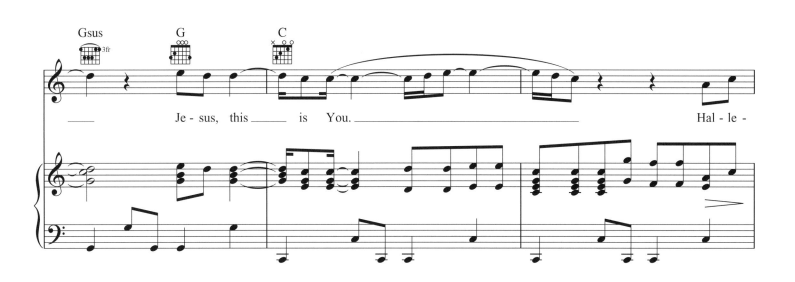

_ Je - sus, this _ is You. _ Hal - le -

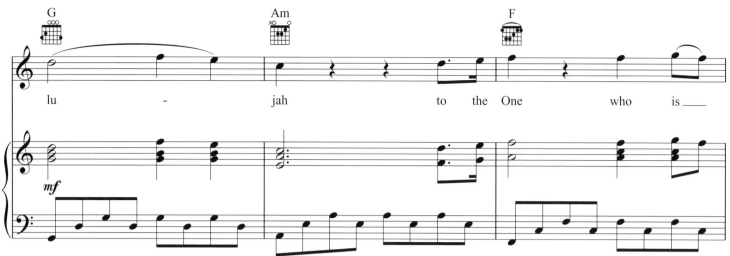

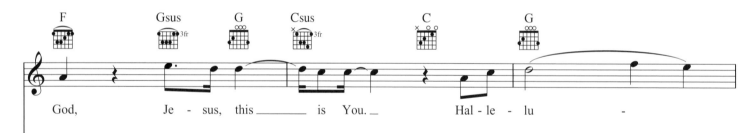

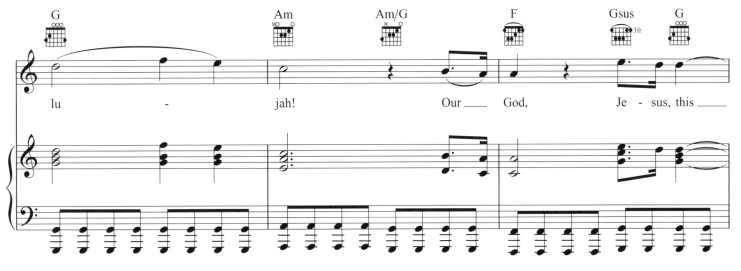

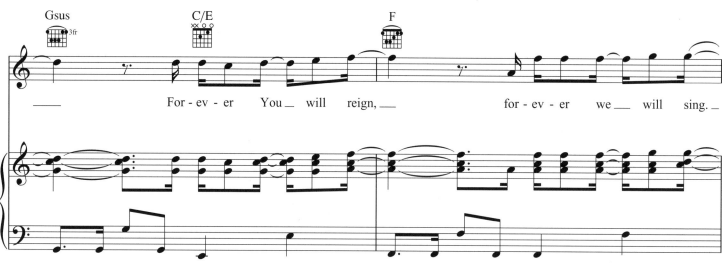

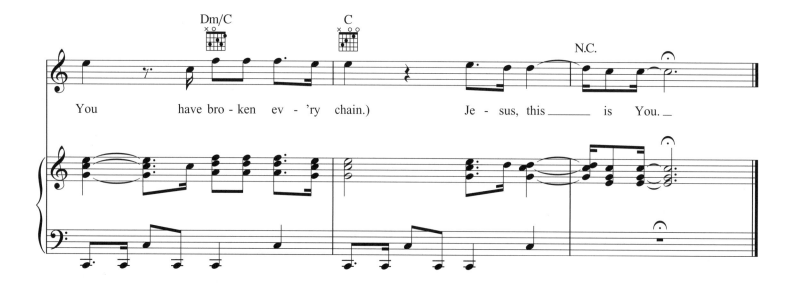